AN
EVERLASTING
NAME

Acknowledgements and copyrights may be found on page 62, which
constitutes an extension of the copyright page.

© Copyright 1991 by Adam Fisher
Published by Behrman House, Inc.
235 Watchung Avenue, West Orange, New Jersey 07052
ISBN 0-87441-515-2

Manufactured in the United States of America

A Service For Remembering The Shoah

AN
EVERLASTING
NAME

Adam Fisher

BEHRMAN HOUSE

Contents

Using this Service 6

A Personal Word 9

Candle Lighting 12

Evening and Morning Service 13

Readings 24

       A. Life Before Shoah 26
       B. The First Shock 28
       C. Ghettos..30
       D. Death Camps 32
       E. Resistance
           I. Spiritual Resistance 34
           II. Ghetto Resistance 34
           III. Death Camp Rebellion and Sabotage 36
           IV. Partisans 37
       F. Abandonment by the World....................................39
       G. Righteous Gentiles 41
       H. Liberation 43
       I. Survivors 45
       J. Rebuilding Lives 48
       K. Implications For Our Time
           I. Jewish Continuity 52
           II. God 53
           III. The Task of Humanity Today 54

Aleinu..57

Yizkor 58

Acknowledgements 62

Using This Service

This service seeks to lovingly remember our people who suffered in the Shoah, to acknowledge their anguish, their struggles, their resistance, the courage of survivors to rebuild their lives, and to bring their voice and our acknowledgement before God. The service also seeks to raise the implications of the Shoah for our time.

Other than my interpretation of the basic prayers, virtually every passage is in the words of those who experienced the Shoah. Some passages are published here for the first time—an added mitzvah of preserving memory.

The English for the Hebrew prayers is an interpretation suggested by the prayer, not a translation.

How to use this service and readings

There are three parts to this book: 1. a liberal evening and morning service; 2. a large selection of readings arranged by topic with clearly marked subdivisions (It is anticipated that only a selection of readings would be used—perhaps one from each of the eleven major divisions.); and 3. a concluding section which includes aleinu, yizkor and kaddish.

The parts of this book might be used in several ways:

a. The service would be followed by a selection of readings and the concluding section.

b. The service would be followed by a speaker without the readings.

c. The congregation's customary service could be used instead of the one provided here. That would be followed by a selection of readings and the concluding section.

d. The readings themselves, are a valuable resource for sermons, classroom discussion, etc. They could be used as a program in itself or following a speaker or some other event discussing or commemorating the Shoah.

e. The music for the songs is found in: *We Are Here*, edited by Eleanor Mlotek and Malke Gottlieb, and *Mir Trogn A Gezang*, edited by Eleanor Mlotek; both published by the Educational Department of the Workmen's Circle, 45 East 33 Street, New York, NY 10016.

When to use this service

1. Holocaust Memorial Day-Yom Hashoah Vehagevurah falls each year on the 27th of Nisan. This is a few days after Passover ends and a week before Israel Independence Day.

2. Anniversary of Kristallnacht, November 9, 1938.

3. Other occasions for remembering the Shoah.

Lights

There are several possibilities regarding the lighting of memorial lights. This is in keeping with lighting yahrzeit candles and lighting lights in the synagogue during yizkor.

One light. Some will choose one light because it represents each individual who suffered and died in their own unique way. Just one light could be placed on a table in front of the congregation, or each participant could be given a candle to light and place in the front of the room before the service begins.

Six lights. Many congregations light six candles in memory of the six million.

Seven lights. Some congregations light six for the six million Jews and one candle for the righteous gentiles or for gentiles who were murdered by the Nazis.

Tzedakah

In the face of the Shoah, one of the questions which we all face is whether we have despaired of redemption for our world and whether we have despaired of God's care in the world. Tzedakah is an affirmation of hope in God and the possibility for redemption. On a more tangible level, it is the commitment to try to alleviate suffering. It is a simple act of caring.

Some may wish to establish a fund for helping Jewish communites which are in danger. Others may wish to broaden the concern to help oppressed people, both Jews and gentiles. Still others may want to help alleviate whatever suffering seems to be the most acute at the time. Rabbi Judah said: "Great is tzedakah in that it brings the redemption

nearer." He also used to say: "Ten hard things have been created in the world. Rock is hard, but iron cleaves it. Iron is hard, but fire softens it. Fire is hard, but water quenches it....Death is the hardest thing of all, but tzedakah overcomes death." (BT Baba Batra 10a)

Names and Memorabilia

Some may want to read names of those murdered in the Shoah. The names may be of relatives of people in the community. Or, 6 (for 6 million) or 18 (for chai meaning life), or 36 (for the legendary 36 righteous who sustain the world) names may be taken from a general list and read during the Yizkor service. For a list of names contact: B'nai B'rith Hillel Foundation, University of Maryland, 7612 Mowatt Lane, P.O. Box 187, College Park, MD 20740- 0187 for "A Memorial of Names." Another source of names is Yad Vashem, P.O. Box 3477, Jerusalem 91034, Israel.

Memorabilia, family photographs and traveling exhibits might be shown during the week prior to Yom Hashoah.

Yellow Tulips

It has been suggested that six yellow tulips be displayed during the service and that vases of yellow tulips be placed in homes. The tulips were chosen because they are the flower of Holland, which along with Denmark, Sweden and Bulgaria, tried to save Jews. The color yellow reminds us of the star Jews were forced to wear. The use of flowers is not part of Jewish mourning customs in modern times, but does have the value of adding a sense of hope when placed alongside a memorial light.

Black Ribbons

Some communities may want to wear black ribbons as a sign of mourning during the service or even for the day.

Appropriate Observance for the day may include viewing films about the Shoah, or supporting some act of social justice. One should refrain from entertainment, holding birthday celebrations, weddings or bar mitzvah celebrations on Yom Hashoah.

Home Observance

This service could be said at home or in the synagogue. In addition, it is appropriate to light a memorial candle and, if desired, to place six yellow tulips near the candle. The following prayer might be said:

The human spirit is the light of God.
As we look at this light,
let us try to imagine six million candles,
each one with the name of another Jew.
Each person was a unique and precious soul,
who struggled and had hope,
who was part of a family,
an orphan, a widow, or widower.
They worked, studied, took walks—
the ordinary things of life.
They celebrated births and weddings,
mourned at funerals.

All were part of the Jewish people,
each was a separate individual.
Each one suffered.
Each and every one was murdered.

May they find rest
under God's sheltering presence.
May their souls find eternal life.
May their memory be for blessing.
Zecher tzadik livracha.

Yom Hashoah Observance–
Further Reading

Noah Golinkin, "How Should We Commemorate the Shoah in Our Homes?" in *Moment*, Vol.14, No. 4, June 1989, p. 30.

Irving Greenberg, *The Jewish Way*, New York, Summit Books, 1988, Chapter 10.

Peter S. Knobel, editor, *Gates of the Seasons*, New York, Central Conference of American Rabbis, 1983, p. 102.

A Personal Word

When I was asked to prepare this service, I considered the project for about a year before I began to work. In time three elements moved me very deeply.

First, it was of paramount importance to me to acknowledge, in as genuine a way as possible, the suffering, struggle, bravery, fear, courage, defeat, humiliation, and anguish of those who experienced the Shoah, and to do so before God. They were individuals who each had their own particular suffering and death or survival. I wanted, to the greatest extent possible, to acknowledge them in their particularity, in addition to their being part of the Jewish people. It is frequently said that we should remember so that it does not happen again. Surely we should do everything in our power so that it does not happen again, but we should remember even if we were somehow assured that it could not happen again. We should remember because those who suffered are part of us, and, in acknowledging them before God we affirm that they and their lives mattered.

Second, a service presents an especially valuable opportunity because it is read on a regular basis, it is both individual and communal, it is connected to the Jewish people, past and present, and it brings all of this into relationship with God.

Since Yom Hashoah is an annual community observance and the liturgy is read each year, a service is one of the main opportunities to bring those first person accounts before people and to make them accessible. There are scores of books with first person accounts of the Shoah. They are indeed precious. But, most Jews do not ordinarily see those books, and the liturgy provides an opportunity to make those accounts accessible.

In the course of the service there is not only a reading of the accounts of the Shoah, but there is public acknowledgement, and acknowledgement before God. In a service, the public acknowledgement is not only given in the contemporary community, but within the context of the history and the destiny of the Jewish people. The connection with God is of great importance because while it is valuable to remember and acknowledge, it is all the more so when done before God who provides the framework of meaning for our lives.

Third, this service is an effort to bring our people's pain, and suffering, and heroism, and endurance before God, but it is not an attempt to solve theological problems. I was determined that the service not attempt to either justify God's apparant silence or reject God, but simply reflect the way in which people actually do relate to God. This service contains a number of passages which equivocate theologically. On one hand, we want to know why God did not protect us. On the other hand, we turn to God for hope in redemption; we praise God for saving the remnant; we say that God has accompanied us in our suffering. The equivocations are purposeful. Most of us, at one time or another, do express these views. Further, I believe that we cannot let go of either end of the theological dilemma created by the Shoah without seriously limiting our relationship with God.

As strongly as I came to feel about these guidelines, there were times when I feared that the acknowledgement would not be true, honest and real. I had the fear that here I am, born in the United States in 1941, without having lost any family in the Shoah, attempting this task. I often wondered if silence would not have been a more prudent response on my part. And yet, the Shoah shapes the consciousness of all Jews, and we all have to listen closely and try to understand what happened. In listening carefully, I tried to provide as honest and as prayerful a service as possible.

It is my prayer, that those who survived the Shoah will indeed find a sense of acknowledgement here, and that the memory of those who were murdered will be appropriately and lovingly honored.

Personal Thanks

Jacob Behrman encouraged me to write and edit this service. I am grateful for this opportunity and for his confidence which has been so important to me.

My thanks to Ruby Strauss, my editor at Behrman House, who has always been supportive, gracious and helpful.

I am grateful to Rabbis Chaim Stern, James Rosenberg, Bonnie Steinberg and Philip Bentley whose extensive comments on the first draft were invaluable. Dr. Stanley Nash, HUC-JIR helped me locate a significant passage of Hebrew poetry.

I wish to acknowledge with deep thanks, the people of Temple Isaiah whose support and encouragement is a source of great blessing, and who have shared the various drafts of this service at Yom Hashoah observances.

My colleague and friend, Cantor Michael Trachtenberg was helpful in selecting the songs.

I am grateful to Betty Yapko who was extremely helpful in the process of obtaining permission from authors and publishers to use their material in this service.

I appreciate the extensive interviews granted by Trude Neu Noack, and Helen and Harry Prus. Siegmar Silber who was brought to England on a kindertransport became my cousin when he was adopted by my great-aunt and uncle after the Shoah. I am grateful to him for his advice and important personal statements which are included here. Allegra Korman and Irving Adler provided extremely valuable written statements. I am grateful to them for their willingness to share their experiences with me. Their words are published here for the first time.

My love and appreciation to my wife, Eileen, whose love and patience has sustained me these twenty-five years. I look forward to dancing with her at our daughters' weddings. I am grateful to her for proofreading the manuscript. For Rachel, whose delight in children brings laughter into the world, and Deborah, whose hands can create whatever artistic vision her heart and mind sees: remember, always remember.

I am grateful to Vic Goldie whose love of language and its music has taught me to listen. He read the manuscript, asked questions and suggested corrections. David Axelrod's friendship and encouragement continues to be important in my work. I am grateful to him for reading the manuscript.

The support of dear friends Steve Hiller, Steve Weitzman and Bob Yarmus continues to enrich my life and work.

The librarians at SUNY Stony Brook and Emma S. Clark Memorial Library, Setauket, N.Y. were always gracious and helpful. My task would have been ever so much more difficult without them and the libraries they serve.

Praised are You, Adonai, the One with whom I walk through the days and nights of my life.

Adam Fisher
Stony Brook, N.Y.

June 1990, Sivan 5750

* *

CANDLE
LIGHTING

* *

EVENING AND
MORNING
SERVICE

* *

Candle Lighting

Before the service begins, the room should be quiet. Those entering are given a yahrzeit or other candle which they are asked to light. These candles can be placed on a table in the front. People then take their seats. Or, at the beginning of the service one candle is lit. Some congregations light six or seven candles.

Six Yellow Tulips. In some congregations six yellow tulips are placed near the candle(s): six, for the six million of our people who were killed; yellow, for the star Jews were forced to wear; tulips, the flower of Holland, which along with Denmark, Sweden and Bulgaria tried to save Jews.

נֵר יְיָ נִשְׁמַת אָדָם

The human spirit is the light of God. As we
look at this light (these lights),
try to imagine six million candles
each one with the name of another Jew.
Each one would signify a unique
      and precious soul,
who struggled and had hope,
who was part of a family,
an orphan, a widow, or a widower.
They worked, studied, took walks—
the ordinary things of life.
They celebrated births and weddings,
mourned at funerals.

All were part of the Jewish people, each one was a separate individual. Each one suffered. Each and every one was murdered.

Evening And Morning Service

Ani Ma'amin

אֲנִי מַאֲמִין בֶּאֱמוּנָה שְׁלֵמָה
בְּבִיאַת הַמָּשִׁיחַ.
וְאַף עַל פִּי שֶׁיִּתְמַהְמֵהַּ,
עִם כָּל זֶה אֲנִי מַאֲמִין,
עִם כָּל זֶה אֲחַכֶּה לוֹ
בְּכָל יוֹם שֶׁיָּבוֹא.

I believe with perfect faith
in the coming of the Messiah,
and despite the long delay
I believe the Messianic time will arrive.

(Moses Maimonides)

Prayer During the Shoah

During the holocaust, three scholars put
God on trial. They felt God was wrong, but,
"after they said it, they all began to pray. To
God. Maybe for God."

(Elie Weisel)

Reader's Kaddish

יִתְגַּדַּל וְיִתְקַדַּשׁ שְׁמֵהּ רַבָּא בְּעָלְמָא דִי
בְרָא כִרְעוּתֵהּ; וְיַמְלִיךְ מַלְכוּתֵהּ בְּחַיֵּיכוֹן
וּבְיוֹמֵיכוֹן, וּבְחַיֵּי דְכָל בֵּית יִשְׂרָאֵל,
בַּעֲגָלָא וּבִזְמַן קָרִיב, וְאִמְרוּ אָמֵן.

יְהֵא שְׁמֵהּ רַבָּא מְבָרַךְ לְעָלַם וּלְעָלְמֵי
עָלְמַיָּא.
יִתְבָּרַךְ וְיִשְׁתַּבַּח, וְיִתְפָּאַר וְיִתְרוֹמַם,
וְיִתְנַשֵּׂא וְיִתְהַדָּר, וְיִתְעַלֶּה וְיִתְהַלָּל שְׁמֵהּ
דְּקֻדְשָׁא, בְּרִיךְ הוּא, לְעֵלָּא מִן כָּל
בִּרְכָתָא וְשִׁירָתָא, תֻּשְׁבְּחָתָא וְנֶחֱמָתָא,
דַּאֲמִירָן בְּעָלְמָא, וְאִמְרוּ אָמֵן.

May God's name be glorified and sanctified
In the world which was created
By the Divine Will.
May God establish sovereignty here below
By your lives, in your days
Soon.
May God send liberation and healing
To give life here on earth.
And may God's rule and the
Divine Name be restored again and say,
    Amen.

May the One who makes peace in the heavens
Bring peace here below.
And may God keep us, those below, in
    close bond
With that Israel which lives on the other side,
Which flourishes as a tree near eternal
    streams.
And answer: Amen.

(Based on "Kaddish," by Aaron Zeitlin)

14

SH'MA AND BLESSINGS

All Rise

בָּרְכוּ אֶת־יְיָ הַמְבֹרָךְ
בָּרוּךְ יְיָ הַמְבֹרָךְ לְעוֹלָם וָעֶד

Praise Adonai, to whom our praise is due.
Praise Adonai, to whom our praise is due,
now and forever.

Night

For an evening service

בָּרוּךְ אַתָּה, יְיָ אֱלֹהֵינוּ, מֶלֶךְ הָעוֹלָם,
אֲשֶׁר בִּדְבָרוֹ מַעֲרִיב עֲרָבִים. בְּחָכְמָה
פּוֹתֵחַ שְׁעָרִים, וּבִתְבוּנָה מְשַׁנֶּה עִתִּים,
וּמַחֲלִיף אֶת הַזְּמַנִּים, וּמְסַדֵּר אֶת
הַכּוֹכָבִים בְּמִשְׁמְרוֹתֵיהֶם בָּרָקִיעַ כִּרְצוֹנוֹ.
בּוֹרֵא יוֹם וָלַיְלָה, גּוֹלֵל אוֹר מִפְּנֵי חֹשֶׁךְ
וְחֹשֶׁךְ מִפְּנֵי אוֹר, וּמַעֲבִיר יוֹם וּמֵבִיא
לַיְלָה, וּמַבְדִּיל בֵּין יוֹם וּבֵין לַיְלָה, יְיָ
צְבָאוֹת שְׁמוֹ. אֵל חַי וְקַיָּם, תָּמִיד
יִמְלוֹךְ עָלֵינוּ, לְעוֹלָם וָעֶד. בָּרוּךְ אַתָּה, יְיָ,
הַמַּעֲרִיב עֲרָבִים.

Our God, creator of the Universe
we come before You in the darkness of
      evening
with memories of a terrifying night,

A night which did "not pass
and a day which did not dawn,"
a time when "the earth was a planet gone bloody,"
      (Shmerke Katcherginsky)

A night when countless numbers of our people
were tortured and murdered.

O God, listen to our memories,
the nightmares of our longest night.

"One can hear the sleepers breathing and
snoring. Many lick their lips and move their
jaws. They are dreaming of eating. You not
only see the food, you feel it in your hands,
you are aware of its rich and striking smell;
someone in the dream holds it up to your lips,
but circumstances prevent the consumption
of the act.

"So our nights drag on. The dreams are woven into indistinct images: the suffering of the day, composed of hunger, blows, cold, exhaustion, fear, turns at nighttime into shapeless nightmares of unheard-of violence. One wakes up at every moment frozen with terror, shaking in every limb. For the whole duration of the night, cutting across the alternating sleep, waking and nightmares, the expectancy and terror of the moment of the reveille keeps watch."

(Primo Levi)

Lord of all worlds
who changes the times and varies the seasons,
who arranges the stars
in their courses in the sky,

Take notice of the long night of suffering when You seemed so distant.

Remember when Israel, God's midnight singer,
perished in a nightmare of darkness.

Morning

For a morning service

בָּרוּךְ אַתָּה, יְיָ אֱלֹהֵינוּ, מֶלֶךְ הָעוֹלָם,
יוֹצֵר אוֹר וּבוֹרֵא חֹשֶׁךְ, עֹשֶׂה שָׁלוֹם,
וּבוֹרֵא אֶת הַכֹּל.
הַמֵּאִיר לָאָרֶץ וְלַדָּרִים עָלֶיהָ בְּרַחֲמִים,
וּבְטוּבוֹ מְחַדֵּשׁ בְּכָל יוֹם תָּמִיד מַעֲשֵׂה
בְרֵאשִׁית. מָה רַבּוּ מַעֲשֶׂיךָ, יְיָ; כֻּלָּם
בְּחָכְמָה עָשִׂיתָ; מָלְאָה הָאָרֶץ קִנְיָנֶךָ.
הַמֶּלֶךְ הַמְרוֹמָם לְבַדּוֹ מֵאָז, הַמְשֻׁבָּח
וְהַמְפֹאָר וְהַמִּתְנַשֵּׂא מִימוֹת עוֹלָם. אֱלֹהֵי
עוֹלָם, בְּרַחֲמֶיךָ הָרַבִּים רַחֵם עָלֵינוּ, אֲדוֹן
עֻזֵּנוּ, צוּר מִשְׂגַּבֵּנוּ, מָגֵן יִשְׁעֵנוּ, מִשְׂגָּב
בַּעֲדֵנוּ. אוֹר חָדָשׁ עַל צִיּוֹן תָּאִיר, וְנִזְכֶּה
כֻלָּנוּ מְהֵרָה לְאוֹרוֹ. בָּרוּךְ אַתָּה, יְיָ, יוֹצֵר
הַמְּאוֹרוֹת.

Our God, Creator of the world
we welcome the morning, and thank You
who creates light and darkness
renewing our world each day.

We welcome morning.
Like a child it brings light and hope.

We come before You with memories
of children from Terezin
who greeted morning too:

"The sun has made a veil of gold
So lovely that my body aches.
Above, the heavens shriek with blue,
Convinced I've smiled by some mistake."

We come before you with memories of children
 who awoke to days of terror:
"The heaviest wheel rolls across our foreheads
To bury itself deep inside our memories.
There's little to eat and much to want," so
"Children steal bread and ask and ask and ask."

"The sun rose over a mount of corpses
And one, who witnessed it, asked:
—Are you not ashamed to rise, sun?"

(H. Leivick)

Our God and Creator
hold our million murdered children
in your memory.

"Perhaps if the sun's tears would sing
against a white stone..."
there would be tears enough
to mourn for them.

(Pavel Friedman and anonymous children)

Let a new light shine on our people.
May the survivors of the Shoah find peace,
no longer plagued by nightmares
and may their children
and their children's children
live without fear,
knowing freedom and contentment.

We praise You, Adonai, our God,
the One who renews creation daily,
the One who makes the sun to rise
and become "a veil of gold."

Torah

Evening

אַהֲבַת עוֹלָם בֵּית יִשְׂרָאֵל עַמְּךָ אָהָבְתָּ,
תּוֹרָה וּמִצְוֹת, חֻקִּים וּמִשְׁפָּטִים, אוֹתָנוּ
לִמָּדְתָּ; עַל כֵּן, יְיָ אֱלֹהֵינוּ, בְּשָׁכְבֵּנוּ
וּבְקוּמֵנוּ נָשִׂיחַ בְּחֻקֶּיךָ, וְנִשְׂמַח בְּדִבְרֵי
תוֹרָתְךָ וּבְמִצְוֹתֶיךָ לְעוֹלָם וָעֶד. כִּי הֵם
חַיֵּינוּ וְאֹרֶךְ יָמֵינוּ, וּבָהֶם נֶהְגֶּה יוֹמָם וָלָיְלָה.
וְאַהֲבָתְךָ אַל תָּסִיר מִמֶּנּוּ לְעוֹלָמִים.
בָּרוּךְ אַתָּה, יְיָ, אוֹהֵב עַמּוֹ יִשְׂרָאֵל.

Morning

אַהֲבָה רַבָּה אֲהַבְתָּנוּ, יְיָ אֱלֹהֵינוּ; חֶמְלָה
גְדוֹלָה וִיתֵרָה חָמַלְתָּ עָלֵינוּ. אָבִינוּ מַלְכֵּנוּ,
בַּעֲבוּר אֲבוֹתֵינוּ שֶׁבָּטְחוּ בְךָ וַתְּלַמְּדֵם חֻקֵּי
חַיִּים, כֵּן תְּחָנֵּנוּ וּתְלַמְּדֵנוּ. אָבִינוּ, הָאָב
הָרַחֲמָן, הַמְרַחֵם, רַחֵם עָלֵינוּ וְתֵן בְּלִבֵּנוּ
לְהָבִין וּלְהַשְׂכִּיל, לִשְׁמֹעַ לִלְמֹד וּלְלַמֵּד,
לִשְׁמֹר וְלַעֲשׂוֹת וּלְקַיֵּם אֶת כָּל דִּבְרֵי
תַלְמוּד תּוֹרָתֶךָ, בְּאַהֲבָה. וְהָאֵר עֵינֵינוּ
בְּתוֹרָתֶךָ, וְדַבֵּק לִבֵּנוּ בְּמִצְוֹתֶיךָ, וְיַחֵד
לְבָבֵנוּ לְאַהֲבָה וּלְיִרְאָה אֶת שְׁמֶךָ, וְלֹא
נֵבוֹשׁ לְעוֹלָם וָעֶד. כִּי בְשֵׁם קָדְשְׁךָ הַגָּדוֹל
וְהַנּוֹרָא בָּטָחְנוּ, נָגִילָה וְנִשְׂמְחָה בִּישׁוּעָתֶךָ.
כִּי אֵל פּוֹעֵל יְשׁוּעוֹת אָתָּה, וְקֵרַבְתָּנוּ
לְשִׁמְךָ הַגָּדוֹל סֶלָה בֶּאֱמֶת, לְהוֹדוֹת לְךָ
וּלְיַחֶדְךָ בְּאַהֲבָה. בָּרוּךְ אַתָּה, יְיָ, הַבּוֹחֵר
בְּעַמּוֹ יִשְׂרָאֵל בְּאַהֲבָה.

Adonai our God, we rejoice in Torah,
the heritage of our ancient partnership
    with You.
The heritage which roots us in history,
and ties us to You.

From Torah we have learned
that we matter in Your sight,
that we are not meaningless specks
in an endless universe,
nor anonymous beings
whose presence in life and history
are of no importance.

From Torah we seek hope and light for our
lives. In Theresienstadt, "We would assemble
in the darkness. To light a candle there, or even
a match, would have brought immediate
disaster upon us. We spoke about matters of
the spirit and eternal questions, about God,
about Jews in the world, about the eternity of
Israel. In the midst of darkness, I sensed light in
the unlit room, the light of Torah."
(Rabbi Leo Baeck)

"This is the holy scripture
in exile
climbing into the sky
with every letter..."
(Nelly Sachs)

We praise You, Adonai our God,
for the heritage of Torah,
and we add our voices
to those who, in life,
proclaimed You One,
who, dying, praised Your Name:

שְׁמַע יִשְׂרָאֵל, יְיָ אֱלֹהֵינוּ, יְיָ אֶחָד.
בָּרוּךְ שֵׁם כְּבוֹד מַלְכוּתוֹ לְעוֹלָם וָעֶד.

Hear O Israel, Adonai is our God,
Adonai is One

May God rule eternally;
may there never be another kingdom
like the holocaust kingdom.

All Are Seated

וְאָהַבְתָּ אֵת יְיָ אֱלֹהֶיךָ בְּכָל לְבָבְךָ
וּבְכָל נַפְשְׁךָ וּבְכָל מְאֹדֶךָ. וְהָיוּ הַדְּבָרִים
הָאֵלֶּה, אֲשֶׁר אָנֹכִי מְצַוְּךָ הַיּוֹם, עַל לְבָבֶךָ.
וְשִׁנַּנְתָּם לְבָנֶיךָ, וְדִבַּרְתָּ בָּם בְּשִׁבְתְּךָ
בְּבֵיתֶךָ, וּבְלֶכְתְּךָ בַדֶּרֶךְ, וּבְשָׁכְבְּךָ
וּבְקוּמֶךָ. וּקְשַׁרְתָּם לְאוֹת עַל יָדֶךָ, וְהָיוּ
לְטֹטָפֹת בֵּין עֵינֶיךָ. וּכְתַבְתָּם עַל מְזֻזוֹת
בֵּיתֶךָ וּבִשְׁעָרֶיךָ.

לְמַעַן תִּזְכְּרוּ וַעֲשִׂיתֶם אֶת־כָּל־מִצְוֹתָי,
וִהְיִיתֶם קְדֹשִׁים לֵאלֹהֵיכֶם. אֲנִי יְיָ
אֱלֹהֵיכֶם, אֲשֶׁר הוֹצֵאתִי אֶתְכֶם מֵאֶרֶץ
מִצְרַיִם לִהְיוֹת לָכֶם לֵאלֹהִים. אֲנִי יְיָ
אֱלֹהֵיכֶם.

You shall love your God with all your heart,
with all your soul and with all your strength.
And you shall take to heart all the words of
Torah which I command you today.

*For Torah guides us to goodness, directs us
away from evil and prods us from indifference. It
teaches us to mend our world—an especially
urgent task after Auschwitz.*

You shall teach them to your children,
and speak of them when you are at home,
and when you are away from home;
when you lie down at night and when you
awaken in the morning.

*You shall commit yourself to the survival of our
people—a mitzvah of compelling importance after
the Shoah.*

You shall bind them for a sign on your
hand, and as a symbol before your eyes. You
shall write them on the doorposts of your
house and on your gates.

*You shall remember and do all My
commandments, and be holy before your God, for
all are responsible to struggle against evil.*

I am Adonai your God. I brought you from
the land of Egypt to be your God. I, Adonai,
am your God.

Alternate Reading:

"You who live safe
In your warm houses,
You who find returning in the evening,
Hot food and friendly faces:
 Consider if this is a man
 Who works in the mud
 Who does not know peace
 Who fights for a scrap of bread
 Who dies because of a yes or a no.
 Consider if this is a woman,
 Without hair and without name
 With no more strength to remember,
 Her eyes empty and her womb cold
 Like a frog in winter.
Meditate that this came about:
I commend these words to you.
Carve them in your hearts
At home, in the street,
Going to bed, rising;
Repeat them to your children,
 Or may your house fall apart,
 May illness impede you,
 May your children turn their faces
  from you."
(Primo Levi)

Redemption of a Remnant

True and certain it is that You are the God
of all the world.

*True and certain it is that Your rule
transcends all tyrants, redeems all suffering.*

After 400 years You redeemed us
    from slavery;
You brought us out of Egypt with a
    mighty hand.

מִי כָמְכָה בָּאֵלִם, יְיָ; מִי כָּמְכָה נֶאְדָּר
בַּקֹּדֶשׁ, נוֹרָא תְהִלֹּת, עֹשֵׂה פֶלֶא.

*Who is like You, Adonai, among the
    mighty?
Who is like You, majestic in holiness, doing
wonders?*

Yet it is said:
There is none like You
among the mute,
remaining silent and keeping still
before those who inflict suffering upon us,
before those who crushed Your people
and burned them.

*Show Your wonders for all to see.
Restore the remnant of Your people
and bring peace upon us once again.*

        (Based on a poem by Yitzchak bar Shalom)

Evening

מַלְכוּתְךָ רָאוּ בָנֶיךָ, בּוֹקֵעַ יָם לִפְנֵי
מֹשֶׁה; "זֶה אֵלִי!" עָנוּ וְאָמְרוּ: "יְיָ יִמְלֹךְ
לְעֹלָם וָעֶד!"

Morning

שִׁירָה חֲדָשָׁה שִׁבְּחוּ גְאוּלִים לְשִׁמְךָ עַל
שְׂפַת הַיָּם; יַחַד כֻּלָּם הוֹדוּ וְהִמְלִיכוּ וְאָמְרוּ:
יְיָ יִמְלֹךְ לְעוֹלָם וָעֶד.

After our people endured unspeakable
    suffering,
God redeemed us and saved us from
    total destruction,
a remnant has survived.

*There is new hope for the Jewish people:
a remnant has returned to the land of Israel,
Jews the world over rejoice in their heritage.*

May You soon fulfill Your promise of
redemption for all the world. Praised are You,
redeemer of Israel.

Evening

וְנֶאֱמַר: "כִּי־פָדָה יְיָ אֶת־יַעֲקֹב, וּגְאָלוֹ
מִיַּד חָזָק מִמֶּנּוּ." בָּרוּךְ אַתָּה, יְיָ, גָּאַל
יִשְׂרָאֵל.

Morning

צוּר יִשְׂרָאֵל, קוּמָה בְּעֶזְרַת יִשְׂרָאֵל,
וּפְדֵה כִנְאֻמְךָ יְהוּדָה וְיִשְׂרָאֵל. גֹּאֲלֵנוּ יְיָ
צְבָאוֹת שְׁמוֹ, קְדוֹשׁ יִשְׂרָאֵל. בָּרוּךְ אַתָּה,
יְיָ, גָּאַל יִשְׂרָאֵל.

TEFILLAH

All rise

God of Abraham and Sarah

בָּרוּךְ אַתָּה, יְיָ אֱלֹהֵינוּ וֵאלֹהֵי אֲבוֹתֵינוּ,
אֱלֹהֵי אַבְרָהָם, אֱלֹהֵי יִצְחָק, וֵאלֹהֵי יַעֲקֹב:
הָאֵל הַגָּדוֹל, הַגִּבּוֹר וְהַנּוֹרָא, אֵל עֶלְיוֹן.
גּוֹמֵל חֲסָדִים טוֹבִים, וְקוֹנֵה הַכֹּל, וְזוֹכֵר
חַסְדֵי אָבוֹת, וּמֵבִיא גְאֻלָּה לִבְנֵי בְנֵיהֶם,
לְמַעַן שְׁמוֹ, בְּאַהֲבָה.
מֶלֶךְ עוֹזֵר וּמוֹשִׁיעַ וּמָגֵן. בָּרוּךְ אַתָּה,
יְיָ, מָגֵן אַבְרָהָם.

Praised are You, Adonai, our God,
and God of Abraham, Isaac and Jacob,
Sarah, Rebecca, Rachel and Leah,

Who remembers the compassion of our ancestors.

Remember the loving kindness of our
people: " In my village, Przedborz, there were
tens of poor shopkeepers who had no money
to buy merchandise for the fair but there were
always people who lent them money. When I

think about those times, I can see how strong
was the desire to help others, to not let anyone
perish from hunger, to help a poor person
celebrate the wedding of a spinster daughter."

(Bronia Davner-Kesselman)

*God of our fathers and mothers, who remembers
the suffering of our people:*

Remember Jacob:
"Firstborn in the grapple of gray morning
where all birth is written with blood
upon the dawn."

(Nelly Sachs)

Remember Rachel who knows
"the place where the end of the way
was torn in flames
from the prophets' bodies."

(Nelly Sachs)

Remember "When the people tried to run
from the Nazis and the crowd finally reached
the large marketplace of Rawa, and there were
no more chances to escape, the German

murderers kept on firing and throwing hand grenades into the crowd."

(Haim Gershonovitz)

Shield of Abraham and Sarah, remember those who perished, remember those who fought, remember those who survived. Remember and protect the people of Israel; remember and bring redemption to their descendents.

Praised are You, Adonai, shield of our people.

Life and Death: A Lasting Fabric

אַתָּה גִבּוֹר לְעוֹלָם, אֲדֹנָי, מְחַיֵּה הַכֹּל
אַתָּה, רַב לְהוֹשִׁיעַ.
מְכַלְכֵּל חַיִּים בְּחֶסֶד, מְחַיֵּה מֵתִים
בְּרַחֲמִים רַבִּים, סוֹמֵךְ נוֹפְלִים, וְרוֹפֵא
חוֹלִים, וּמַתִּיר אֲסוּרִים, וּמְקַיֵּם אֱמוּנָתוֹ
לִישֵׁנֵי עָפָר. מִי כָמוֹךָ, בַּעַל גְּבוּרוֹת, וּמִי
דוֹמֶה לָךְ, מֶלֶךְ מֵמִית וּמְחַיֶּה וּמַצְמִיחַ
יְשׁוּעָה.
וְנֶאֱמָן אַתָּה לְהַחֲיוֹת מֵתִים. בָּרוּךְ
אַתָּה יְיָ, נֹטֵעַ בְּתוֹכֵנוּ חַיֵּי עוֹלָם.

Adonai, You bind the living and the dead together in a lasting fabric.

You renew life beyond death, You keep faith with those who sleep in the dust. Keep faith with parents and children.

Keep faith, O God, with Arthur Neu. His daughter remembers: "Before the Shoah, every Friday night my father went to the synagogue, came home and made kiddush. When I was a little girl he took my hand and we walked around the room singing Shalom Aleichem."

(Trude Neu Noack)

Keep faith, O God, with this child and her father.

Keep faith, O God, with those who were murdered at Treblinka: "At the gas chamber I was chosen to work there as a barber. The Germans needed the women's hair for their purposes. They told us 'make all those women believe that they are just taking a haircut.' We already knew that this room was the last place they went in alive. Some of the women that came in on a transport from my town...I knew them; I lived with them in my town. And when they saw me, they started asking me, 'Abe, What's going to happen to us?' What could you tell them?"

(Abraham Bomba)

Adonai our God, keep faith with those who sleep in the dust. Bind them to You and to us in a lasting fabric.

Holiness

Evening:

אַתָּה קָדוֹשׁ וְשִׁמְךָ קָדוֹשׁ, וּקְדוֹשִׁים
בְּכָל יוֹם יְהַלְלוּךָ סֶּלָה.

Morning:

נְקַדֵּשׁ אֶת שִׁמְךָ בָּעוֹלָם כְּשֵׁם
שֶׁמַּקְדִּישִׁים אוֹתוֹ בִּשְׁמֵי מָרוֹם, כַּכָּתוּב
עַל יַד נְבִיאֶךָ: וְקָרָא זֶה אֶל זֶה וְאָמַר:
קָדוֹשׁ, קָדוֹשׁ, קָדוֹשׁ יְיָ צְבָאוֹת; מְלֹא
כָל הָאָרֶץ כְּבוֹדוֹ.
לְעֻמָּתָם בָּרוּךְ יֹאמֵרוּ —
בָּרוּךְ כְּבוֹד יְיָ מִמְּקוֹמוֹ.
וּבְדִבְרֵי קָדְשְׁךָ כָּתוּב לֵאמֹר:
יִמְלֹךְ יְיָ לְעוֹלָם, אֱלֹהַיִךְ צִיּוֹן לְדֹר וָדֹר;
הַלְלוּיָהּ.

You are holy, Your name is holy
and Your creation praises You daily.
You are holy, and human beings,
each one created in Your image,
contain a spark of your holiness.

Dear God of holiness, remember
those in ghettos and death camps
who knew that life is holy
and did simple acts of kindness.

"Ilse, a childhood friend of mine, once found
a raspberry in the camp and carried it in her
pocket all day to present to me that night on a
leaf. Imagine a world in which your entire
possession is one raspberry, and you give it to
your friend."

(Gerda Weissmann Klein)

O God of holiness, remember
those in ghettos and death camps
who knew that life is holy,
yet took their own lives
rather than cooperate
in the killing of their people.

Adam Czerniakow, president of the Jewish
Council of Warsaw, realized that there was no
future for the ghetto: the Jews would be killed.
By 4:00 P.M. on July 22, 1940 he was to have
6,000 men, women and children chosen for
"transport" to the east. "He is terribly worried
that the orphans will be deported and
repeatedly brings up the orphans. If he cannot
take care of the orphans, then he has lost his
war, he has lost his struggle." He killed
himself on July 23.

(Raul Hilberg)

Dear God of holiness, remember
those who knew that life is holy
and rebelled against those
who inflicted death.

Prisoners who met the trains at Auschwitz
"would give warnings: 'Do something! Fight!
Fight back while you have the strength!' In
September 1944, there was a plan to blow up
the gas chambers. There was a small Krupp
factory nearby. Prisoners smuggled
explosives, powder and small arms. The men

working in the gas chamber started to blow up
the gas chambers. Two were destroyed."

(Jack Goldman)

Holy One of Israel, remember
all those in ghettos and death camps
who knew that life is holy.
Praised are You, Adonai,
the Holy One of Israel.

Evening:

בָּרוּךְ אַתָּה, יְיָ, הָאֵל הַקָּדוֹשׁ.

Morning:

לְדוֹר וָדוֹר נַגִּיד גָּדְלֶךָ, וּלְנֵצַח נְצָחִים
קְדֻשָּׁתְךָ נַקְדִּישׁ, וְשִׁבְחֲךָ אֱלֹהֵינוּ מִפִּינוּ
לֹא יָמוּשׁ לְעוֹלָם וָעֶד, כִּי אֵל מֶלֶךְ גָּדוֹל
וְקָדוֹשׁ אָתָּה. בָּרוּךְ אַתָּה יְיָ, הָאֵל הַקָּדוֹשׁ.

All are seated

Remember The Shoah: Mourn, Seek Comfort and Hope in Renewal

Adonai our God, comfort us on this day of
remembering the Shoah.

Comfort all of us who are mourners for our
people.

✳   ✳

Choose one or more of the following:

Cracow. "In Cracow on December 5, 1939,
my uncle Maximilian Redlich was taken to the
synagogue on Isaacs Street and ordered to set
fire to the Scrolls of the Law. When my uncle
refused he was promptly shot and killed."

(Julian Gross)

Maidanek. "I spent two weeks in Maidanek.
Every day during roll call, young women were
ushered into the gas chambers. If one had a
bandaged leg, or had blisters as a result of

sunburn, or a simple sore, or was too tired to report for roll call, she was doomed."

(Esther Garfinkel was an inmate of Maidanek where her two children were killed.)

Sobibor. "(At first,) the bodies weren't burned, they were buried. In early January 1944 we (were forced to) began digging up the bodies (to be burned). When the last mass grave was opened, I recognized my whole family. Mom and my sisters. Three sisters with their kids. They were all in there."

(Motke Zaidl)

* *

We mourn for murdered families and
   friends.
We mourn for those we do not even know
but who are part of us.

"The lightnings of sorrow do not allow
The field of forgetting to fall asleep."
(Nelly Sachs)

"The blossoms of comfort are too small
Not enough for the torment of a child's tear."
(Nelly Sachs)

Will the Lord desert us forever
showing us favor
no more?
(Ps. 77:9)

The Holy One said to Moses: "Do you not think that I am in pain just as Israel is in pain? I share in Israel's sufferings." This is why it is said in Isaiah, "In all their afflictions God was afflicted."

(Exodus Rabbah II.5)

Adonai, remember and take heed.
May You be the comforter of Zion,
the rebuilder of Your people.

Adonai, remove grief and suffering from us. Grant healing for all our wounds.

Sound the shofar for our freedom
and redeem our people.

I will seek out My flock, I will rescue them from
all the places to which they were scattered. I will
bring them to their own land. I will bandage the
injured and I will sustain the weak.
(Ezek. 34)

Israel. "We have gathered up human particles and combined them into the fruitful and creative nucleus of a nation revived. We have built villages and towns, planted gardens and established factories. We have breathed new life into our muted and abandoned ancient language. Such a marvel is unique in the history of human culture."

(Attributed to David Ben Gurion)

America. "We opened up a business. Our kids went to yeshiva and college. Look what we accomplished. After all, we are strangers in the land, but we tried our best and raised a good family."

(Helen and Harry Prus)

"If the Jewish people can survive a Holocaust, they can turn from sorrow and toward rejoicing."
(Siegmar Koppold Silber)

Our Prayers and Memories

רְצֵה, יְיָ אֱלֹהֵינוּ, בְּעַמְּךָ יִשְׂרָאֵל,
וּתְפִלָּתָם בְּאַהֲבָה תְקַבֵּל, וּתְהִי לְרָצוֹן
תָּמִיד עֲבוֹדַת יִשְׂרָאֵל עַמֶּךָ. בָּרוּךְ אַתָּה,
יְיָ, שָׁאוֹתְךָ לְבַדְּךָ בְּאַהֲבָה נַעֲבוֹד.

God of our fathers and mothers,
may our prayers and the memories
which we place before You this day
be worthy in Your sight
and in the sight of our people
who suffered in the Shoah.

Thankfulness

מוֹדִים אֲנַחְנוּ לָךְ, שָׁאַתָּה הוּא יְיָ
אֱלֹהֵינוּ וֵאלֹהֵי אֲבוֹתֵינוּ לְעוֹלָם וָעֶד. צוּר
חַיֵּינוּ, מָגֵן יִשְׁעֵנוּ אַתָּה הוּא. לְדוֹר וָדוֹר
נוֹדֶה לְךָ, וּנְסַפֵּר תְּהִלָּתֶךָ, עַל חַיֵּינוּ
הַמְּסוּרִים בְּיָדֶךָ, וְעַל נִשְׁמוֹתֵינוּ הַפְּקוּדוֹת
לָךְ, וְעַל נִסֶּיךָ שֶׁבְּכָל יוֹם עִמָּנוּ, וְעַל
נִפְלְאוֹתֶיךָ וְטוֹבוֹתֶיךָ שֶׁבְּכָל עֵת, עֶרֶב
וָבֹקֶר וְצָהֳרָיִם. הַטּוֹב כִּי לֹא כָלוּ רַחֲמֶיךָ,
וְהַמְרַחֵם כִּי לֹא תַמּוּ חֲסָדֶיךָ, מֵעוֹלָם
קִוִּינוּ לָךְ.

וְעַל כֻּלָּם יִתְבָּרַךְ וְיִתְרוֹמַם שִׁמְךָ,
מַלְכֵּנוּ, תָּמִיד לְעוֹלָם וָעֶד.
וְכֹל הַחַיִּים יוֹדוּךָ סֶּלָה, וִיהַלְלוּ אֶת
שִׁמְךָ בֶּאֱמֶת, הָאֵל, יְשׁוּעָתֵנוּ וְעֶזְרָתֵנוּ
סֶלָה. בָּרוּךְ אַתָּה, יְיָ, הַטּוֹב שִׁמְךָ, וּלְךָ
נָאֶה לְהוֹדוֹת.

God of our fathers and mothers, we have asked,
"Has God forgotten how to pity?" (Ps. 77.10)
and yet we acknowledge that You
are the foundation of our lives and our hope,
and we thank You for Your wonders
which we experience each day.

We thank You for the remnant which
  has survived,
for those who built the land of Israel,
for those who nurture Jewish life in all lands.

Peace

Evening

שָׁלוֹם רָב עַל יִשְׂרָאֵל עַמְּךָ תָּשִׂים
לְעוֹלָם, כִּי אַתָּה הוּא מֶלֶךְ אָדוֹן לְכָל
הַשָּׁלוֹם, וְטוֹב בְּעֵינֶיךָ לְבָרֵךְ אֶת עַמְּךָ

יִשְׂרָאֵל בְּכָל עֵת וּבְכָל שָׁעָה בִּשְׁלוֹמֶךָ.
בָּרוּךְ אַתָּה, יְיָ, הַמְבָרֵךְ אֶת עַמּוֹ יִשְׂרָאֵל
בַּשָּׁלוֹם.

Morning

שִׂים שָׁלוֹם, טוֹבָה וּבְרָכָה, חֵן וָחֶסֶד
וְרַחֲמִים, עָלֵינוּ וְעַל כָּל יִשְׂרָאֵל עַמֶּךָ.
בָּרְכֵנוּ אָבִינוּ, כֻּלָּנוּ כְּאֶחָד, בְּאוֹר פָּנֶיךָ; כִּי
בְאוֹר פָּנֶיךָ נָתַתָּ לָּנוּ, יְיָ אֱלֹהֵינוּ, תּוֹרַת
חַיִּים וְאַהֲבַת חֶסֶד, וּצְדָקָה וּבְרָכָה
וְרַחֲמִים, וְחַיִּים וְשָׁלוֹם. וְטוֹב בְּעֵינֶיךָ
לְבָרֵךְ אֶת עַמְּךָ יִשְׂרָאֵל בְּכָל עֵת וּבְכָל
שָׁעָה בִּשְׁלוֹמֶךָ. בָּרוּךְ אַתָּה, יְיָ, הַמְבָרֵךְ
אֶת עַמּוֹ יִשְׂרָאֵל בַּשָּׁלוֹם.

God of our fathers and mothers,
bless the remnant of Your people Israel,
with peace and well being
in the land of Israel and in every land
where they are found.
May they be disciples of Aaron,
bringing peace and justice into the world.

Silent Prayer

יִהְיוּ לְרָצוֹן אִמְרֵי־פִי וְהֶגְיוֹן לִבִּי לְפָנֶיךָ,
יְיָ, צוּרִי וְגוֹאֲלִי.

May the words I have spoken and the
contemplations of my heart be acceptable
before You and before those who have
suffered in the Shoah.

or

עֹשֶׂה שָׁלוֹם בִּמְרוֹמָיו, הוּא יַעֲשֶׂה
שָׁלוֹם עָלֵינוּ וְעַל־כָּל־יִשְׂרָאֵל, וְאִמְרוּ אָמֵן.

May the One who brings peace to reign on
high, bring peace and fulfillment to us, to
Israel and the world.

READINGS

*I will give them an
everlasting name"*

(Isa.56.5)

*"There were
messages I had to
deliver to the living
from the dead to
show what I have
lived through, on
behalf of the millions
who had seen it
also—but could no
longer speak."*

(Eugene Heimler)

Read one or more of the readings in at least several areas.

A. Life Before Shoah..26
B. The First Shock 28
C. Ghettos...30
D. Death Camps...32
E. Resistance
    I. Spiritual Resistance...34
    II. Ghetto Resistance 34
    III. Death Camp Rebellion and Sabotage........36
    IV. Partisans...37
F. Abandonment by the World 39
G. Righteous Gentiles 41
H. Liberation 43
I. Survivors 45
J. Rebuilding Lives..48
K. Implications For Our Time
    I. Jewish Continuity 52
    II. God 53
    III. The Task of Humanity Today 54

Prayers are said before and after the collection of readings.

Prayer Before Readings

We come before You, our God, bearing the words of witnesses,
that the preciousness of their lives before the Shoah,
the anguish of their suffering during it,
the courage of those who resisted
and the resolve of those who rebuilt their lives,
might live on in Your Eternity.

Let us lovingly remember their lives
and give them a voice,
an eternal name.

THE LIVES OF EUROPEAN JEWS
BEFORE THE SHOAH

Trude Noack was born in Langen, Germany which is a small town near Frankfort in which there were 25 Jewish families in a population of ten thousand. Her father sold leather and other supplies to shoemakers.

Family Life
"What gave my parents the most joy in life was family and being Jewish. They saved for the future and once in a blue moon went to the theater. Every so often if there was someone in the shul who wasn't from the town and didn't have a place—migrants who came from eastern Europe—my father would bring them home for dinner on Friday night. One day a week my mother went to Frankfort and met with her sister and her father. My grandfather would take me to the conditterai—the pastery shop—and I got to eat the whipped cream. Once a week—it was a ritual."

Friends
"On Sundays a few of us friends would get together and ride our bicycles to a nearby town. We would go in the morning and we came back in the afternoon. The others could eat out but the Jewish kids had to take sandwiches from home because we kept kosher and couldn't eat in a restaurant. We all got along fine. We were very much part of the group."

(Trude Noack came alone to the U.S. in November 1937. Her entire family was killed except for her mother, who survived.)

Maurice Meier first settled in Griessen, Germany in 1919 and started farming. In 1923 he married Martha Abraham. In 1926 he bought a farm in Tiengen.

Newlyweds Welcomed
"We were the only Jews in the community (Griessen), but from the very beginning we lived in happy association with our Christian neighbors. On our return from our wedding trip we found our house decorated with garlands and a banner with the greeting 'Welcome and God bless you.' In the house we

found our table spread with Black Forest bread and cheese. In the evening we were serenaded, according to the Black Forest custom, by the town band, directed by the clerk of the town council."

Hopes

"Tiengen was a peaceful and pleasant place in those days, a busy center of commerce by day, an idyllic rural village in the evening. It was a prosperous domain which we had developed in the hope and expectation that it would be a home not only for us but also for our children."

Jewish Life

"Unlike most villages of its kind in Germany, Tiengen had a synagogue with a fairly large Jewish congregation. The sight of men in shiny silk top-hats walking through the streets to the synagogue on Saturday mornings with their wives and children is a vivid recollection in the mind of anyone who knew Tiengen."

> (After the Nazis usurped power, the Meier family fled to Switzerland and then to France. Maurice Meier was sent to a detention camp where he suffered a total loss of hearing. He later escaped to Switzerland. After the war he learned that his entire family had been exterminated.)

Harry and Helen Prus grew up in small towns in Poland.

Harry Prus: "There were about 1,200 Jews and several thousand others in our town (Kroszniewice). I went to Yeshiva and also had private tutors. We had a wholesale grocery business. It was a big business and we made a good living. I had two brothers and everybody worked in the business. We didn't have pogroms or anything. Poland was independent and a democracy at that time.

"I was supposed to get married. The father of the girl would have taken me in and given me a big building. I was supposed to be something. My brother was preparing to go to Israel."

Helen Prus: "In Stashov there were about 4,000 Jews and 4,000 others. Our town had more cultural life and an intelligentsia. I went to public school with Polish children. The anti-semitism was unbelievable. We sat separately. The Polish children sat on one side and we sat on the other side. Every morning the Polish girls stood up to say their prayers (I even remember the prayer), and we stood up with them. We were silent. They had one hour of religion which we did not attend. They went to school six days, but we only went five days because of Shabbat. We went to them and they gave us the homework.

"Even before the war we knew there was no future. A lot of people emigrated to the United States or Canada. All the Zionist organizations planned to go to Israel, but we never thought of going any place. I was eager to learn things and joined the Zionist movement with my friends. My background was very religious. I went to Beis Yaakov, and my mother was very much against my going to Zionist meetings. She punished me terribly. Some parents threw their children out of the house for being involved with Zionist groups.

"We were very friendly with the Poles, but they were anti-semites. They were jealous of us because we lived nicer than them. It was friendly on top but if they got drunk—on Sunday night they got drunk—we were afraid to go out. They were always cursing the Jews: 'Go to Palestine! Dirty Jews! Christ Killers!' But there were no pogroms."

> (Harry and Helen Prus survived concentration camps and were married in Bergen Belsen. They now live in the United States.)

1933-THE FIRST SHOCK

Trude Noack of Langen, Germany
Social Isolation

"On the other side of the street there was a public school. The custodian who had been there ever since I can remember, lost his job because he didn't join the Nazi party. A terrible Nazi, the black sheep of his family, by the name of Peter Searing got the job. He was in all kinds of trouble and could never keep a job. From that day on, everyone was afraid to talk to us because he threatened the other people. They couldn't speak to us openly. I had a friend (her father worked for the bank) who used to pick me up and we'd go to school together. Within a week of when Hitler came to power on March 5th, her mother called my mother to say that she couldn't pick me up any more because they were afraid her husband would lose his job. Within a week, Ruth, the other Jewish girl, and I were treated like we had the plague. Nobody talked to us."

> (Trude Noack was sent to the U.S. by her parents in 1937. Her father perished in a concentration camp but her mother survived because she was hidden by a Christian family in Belgium.)

Maurice Meier of Tiengen, Germany

Intimidation

"The first hint that there was anything amiss came unexpectedly one morning in the early spring of 1933. All street intersections in Tiengen and in the vicinity were occupied by storm troopers. Felix, our hired man, received a telegram urging him to leave us

immediately; our day laborer, Thomas, telephoned in the evening to say that he could not come to work. Brigitte, the maid of some friends of ours, was in our kitchen crouching in a corner, crying, trembling with fear. She was a Christian girl who had been employed in a Jewish home for many years. She had been accosted by some of the local brown-shirts who told her that she must leave her Jewish employer. When she had refused they said that they would come and get her on Saturday and would publicly cut off her hair and shave her head. Now she was afraid to go to her house and begged us to hide her.

"In the course of the day some of our non-Jewish friends, disregarding the dangers of being photographed and marked as Jew lovers, came to visit us."

Humiliation in School

"Day after day, Ernst (our son) was humiliated and insulted in one way or another by the teacher, but, for a long time there was strangely enough no change in the attitude and conduct of the other children toward him.

"Toward the end of May the teacher had read off the names of the pupils who were to go on the school picnic, omitting Ernst's name. At the end of the roll call he looked at Ernst and said, 'Jews are not wanted at our picnic.' Ernst stepped out of line, but the teacher shouted to the children, 'Boys, get him and knock out of him any ideas he may have about coming to our school anymore.' Several rowdies attacked him and soon the whole class was beating him with the teacher gleefully shouting his enouragement. I went to the principal of the school. He listened sympathetically and said, 'I am truly sorry for you and for Ernst, but I cannot do a thing because Ernst's teacher is a party member.'"

Fleeing the Mob

"One of our non-Jewish neighbors came to our house and said, 'There's a big mob of rowdies making a demonstration in front of H's house because he criticized the Fuhrer and said there was no power on earth that was as strong as his Christian faith. The SS is on its way to arrest H and take him to Dachau. He's left the house and is hiding. He's on the Nazi list just as you are.' At a distance from H's house we could hear the hysterical mob, 'Lynch him...' Terrified, I went to kiss the children good bye. I drove quickly to the bridge and in few minutes I was safely across the border in Switzerland. That night two men from Tiengen were taken away to Dachau."

> (Maurice Meier survived, but his family was exterminated.)

Helen Prus, Stashovl, Poland

"Already in 1933 there were campaigns not to buy from Jews. I decided to join the Shomer Hatzair Zionists even though I came from a religious family. They were smarter than the religious Jews who believed that the messiah will come and take them to Israel; as long as you believe in God everything will be all right. We used to get together and try to think of ways to defend ourselves. In 1939 many went into the woods to escape.

"Hitler came into Poland in 1939. In 1940 we were arrested and pushed into a ghetto. When we were forced to leave our homes, the Poles were standing in the streets and pointing at us and calling out, 'Before the houses were yours and the streets were ours, but now the streets are yours and the houses are ours.' They called out threats: 'They will make soap out of you. They'll take your hair and make brushes out of it.' These were our friends and neighbors?"

> (Helen Prus survived Bergen Belsen, met and married Harry in a DP camp, and gave birth to twins there. They now live in the United States.)

Song: Gib A Brokhe Tsu Dayn Kind *Mother, Send a Blessing For Your Child*

> (Sung by deported Jews from Cracow. Author and composer unknown.)

Ikh gedenk vos iz demolt geven,
Eyn tog der vayser herlekh un sheyn,
Un mayn mame iz bay der kikh farnumen,
Di shvester, di kleyne, iz arayngekumen.

Zi hot gehert a nayes haynt af der gas
Az morgn fri vet a registratsye zayn,
As yunge mener biz finf un draysik yor
Muzn morgn baym arbetsamt shteyn.

> Mame, mame blayb gezunt.
> Avek fun dir muz ikh atsind.
> Az got vet gebn
> Gezunt un lebn
> Veln mir zikh zen gezunt.

I recall how it all took place,
That last day had a pleasant pace.
There my mother stood occupied,
My youngest sister flies inside—
On the street she heard the news
That registration is the command,
That all young men up to thirty-five
Must in the labor task-force stand.

> Mother, mother, farewell I say,
> I must leave you, go away.
> If God will give
> Good health, we'll live,
> See each other soon, I pray.

GHETTOS

Jacob Celemenski, Menzerzyce:
Rabbi Murdered

(Jacob Celemenski was born in Warsaw in 1904. He was sent to Auschwitz in 1944 and made his way to America in 1950.)

"As a courier of the underground, I carried aid and the forbidden Jewish printed word to Jews confined in ghettos and camps.

"I remember the town of Menzerzyce from prewar days. I was familiar with its marketplace and its charming streets lined with small wooden or brick houses. It had a large population of Jewish workers.

"Mordekai Honey sat down across the table from me and said, 'You've come at a bad time. Something terrible happened here yesterday.' He told me that the Gestapo had shot the rabbi in the street the day before. The rabbi, a small, hunchbacked man, was famed for his learning and kindness. The Germans had wanted to deport him, but he refused to deliver himself into their hands and went into hiding. The Gestapo then took twenty-five of the town's Jews as hostages and announced that they would all be shot if 'the Jews' failed to surrender. As soon as he learned of this, the rabbi went to the Gestapo. He was tortured, and later taken out into the street and shot. The whole town was crushed and heartsick over it."

Peter Fischel, Terezin:
Hunger and Death

(Peter Fischel, 15 yrs. old, perished in Auschwitz in 1944.)

"We got used to standing in line at 7 o'clock in the morning, at 12 noon and again at seven o'clock in the evening. We stood in a long queue with a plate in our hand, into which they ladled a little warmed-up water with a salty or a coffee flavor. Or else they gave us a few potatoes. We got used to sleeping without a bed, to saluting every uniform, not to walk on the sidewalks and then again to walk on the sidewalks. We got used to undeserved slaps, blows and executions. We got accustomed to seeing people die in their own excrement, to seeing piled-up coffins full of corpses, to seeing the sick amidst dirt and filth and to seeing the helpless doctors. We got used to it that from time to time, one thousand unhappy souls would come here and that, from time to time, another thousand unhappy souls would go away."

Bernard Goldstein, Warsaw:
Death, Music

(Bernard Goldstein was a leader of the General Socialist Labor Organization. He joined the underground and survived the destruction of the Warsaw ghetto.)

The Dead

"The year is 1941. Typhus rages in the ghetto, taking a monthly toll of six to seven thousand. It is dawn. In a courtyard on Mila Street the cobblestones are strewn with naked corpses that are covered with dirty paper. There is no money for burial."

Music

"A cacophony of wailing, of crying , of moaning and of shrieking fills the air. And, in the midst of all this, one suddenly hears the sound of music, of singing, of symphonic music and of jazz. The music emanates from a courtyard at the end of the street. A group consisting of former actors, singers, musicians, choristers, members of the Philharmonic of days gone by, is trying to eke out a bleak livelihood, a bit of bread, by singing in the streets and in the courtyards. People drop a few coins into outstretched caps and plates.

The performers thank them sullenly, and move on, singing:

> Poverty leaps,
> Poverty dances,
> Poverty sings a little song."

Primo Levi, Fossoli, Italy: Detention Camp, February 1944

(Primo Levi was a chemist. He survived Auschwitz, returned to Italy, and wrote several important books on the holocaust.)

Preparing to Leave

"On the morning of the 21st we learned that on the following day the Jews would be leaving. For every person missing at the roll call, ten would be shot.

"All took leave from life in the manner which most suited them. Some praying, some deliberately drunk, others lustfully intoxicated for the last time. But the mothers stayed up to prepare the food for the journey with tender care and washed their children and packed the luggage; and at dawn the barbed wire was full of children's washing hung out in the wind to dry. Would you not do the same? If you and your child were going to be killed tomorrow, would you not give him to eat today?"

Tripoli Women Mourn

"When all was ready, the food cooked, the bundles tied together, (the women in the Gattegno family from Tripoli) unloosened their hair, took off their shoes, placed the Yahrzeit candles on the ground and lit them according to the customs of their fathers, and sat on the bare soil in a circle for the lamentations, praying and weeping all night.

"Dawn came on us like a betrayer; it seemed as though the new sun rose as an ally of our enemies to assist in our destruction.

"They then loaded us on to the buses and took us to the station of Capri. Here the train was waiting for us."

Song: Shtiler, Shtiler Quiet, Quiet

(This is a song of the Vilna ghetto. An eleven-year-old boy, Alex Wolkoviski, wrote this prize-winning melody in a ghetto contest. He is now a composer, called Tamir, in Israel. Shmerke Kaczerginski set words to the tune.)

Shtiler, shtiler, lomir shvaygn,
Kvorim vaksn do.
S'hobn zey farflantst di sonim:
Grinen zey tsum blo.
S'firn vegn tsu ponar tsu,
S'firt keyn veg tsurik,
Iz der tate vu farshvundn
Un mit im dos glik.
Shtiler, kind mayns, veyn nit, oyster,
S'helft nit keyn geveyn,
Undzer umglik veln sonim
Say vi nit farshteyn.
S'hobn breges oykh di yamen,
S'hobn tfises oykhet tsamen,
Nor tsu undzer payn
Keyn bisl shayn,
Keyn bisl shayn.

Quiet, Quiet, let's be silent,
Dead are growing here.
They were planted by the tyrant,
See their bloom appear.
All the roads lead to Ponar now,
There are no roads back,
And your father too has vanished,
And with him our luck.
Still, my child, don't cry, my jewel,
Tears no help commands,
Our pain callous people
Never understand.
Seas and oceans have their order,
Prison also has its border,
But to our plight
There is no light,
There is no light.

DEATH CAMPS

Nobody Knows The Count

The final solution:
they wanted to
exterminate
the Jews to have
a Pure race.
Definitely. It
was definitely
the Jews. It
was directed at
the Jews. They
annihilated
six million
Jews. God Knows
the actual count,
Nobody knows
the count.

> (From an American soldier who liberated the death camps.)

O The Chimneys

"And though after my skin destroy this
body, yet in my flesh shall I see God."
  Job 19.26
O the chimneys
On the ingeniously devised habitations of
  death
When Israel's body drifted as smoke
Through the air—
Was welcomed by a star, a chimney sweep,
A star that turned black
Or was it a ray of sun?

O the chimneys!
Freedomway for Jeremiah and Job's dust—
Who devised you and laid stone upon stone
The road for refugees of smoke?

O the habitations of death,
Invitingly appointed
For the host who used to be a guest—
O you fingers
Laying the threshold
Like a knife between life and death—

O you chimneys,
O you fingers
And Israel's body as smoke through the air!

> (Nelly Sachs fled to Sweden from Germany in 1940. She received the Nobel Prize for Literature in 1966.)

"After Arriving At The Camp...

...for the first time, we became aware that our language lacks words to express this offense, the demolition of a man. In a moment, with almost prophetic intuition the reality was revealed to us: we had reached the bottom. It is not possible to sink lower than this; no human condition is more miserable than this, nor could it conceivably be so. Nothing belongs to us any more; they have taken away our clothes, our shoes, even our hair; if we speak, they will not listen to us, and if they listen, they will not understand. They will even take away our name: and if we want to keep it, we will have to find ourselves the strength to do so, to manage somehow so that behind the name, something of us, of us as we were, still remains.

"I have learnt that I am a Haftling (Prisoner). My number is 174517; we will carry the tattoo on our left arm until we die."

> (Primo Levi, an Italian chemist, survived Auschwitz and wrote several important books on the Shoah.)

Shoes

"Death begins with the shoes; for most of us, they show themselves to be instruments of torture, which after a few hours of marching cause painful sores which become fatally infected. Whoever has them arrives last everywhere, and everywhere he receives blows. His feet swell and the more they swell, the more friction with the wood and cloth of the shoes become insupportable. Then only the hospital is left: but to enter the hospital with a diagnosis of "dicke Fusse" (swollen feet) is extremely dangerous, because it is well known to all, and especially to the SS, that here there is no cure for that complaint."

(Primo Levi)

Bread

"The distribution of bread, of the holy gray slab which seems gigantic in your neighbor's hand, and in your own hand so small as to make you cry. It is a daily hallucination to which in the end one becomes accustomed: but at the beginning it is so irresistible that many of us, after long discussions on our own open and constant misfortune and the shameless luck of others, finally exchange our ration, at which the illusion is renewed inverted, leaving everyone discontented and frustrated."

(Primo Levi)

The Silent Partner

Three meters wide
six meters deep and fifteen meters long—
these are the measurements of one of the pits
in Poland
to which the Germans drove Jews—
shot them there
and buried them.
Three meters wide
six meters deep
and fifteen meters long—
the three dimensions.
And the fourth dimension,
the one in which all the slaughtered Jews
cannot die
and cannot live—

is now the silent partner
through all the days of my life.

(Rajzel Zychlinsky fled from Poland to the East. The Nazis slaughtered the rest of her family. In 1951 she came to New York.)

Gas Chamber, Auschwitz

"As people reached the crematorium, they saw everything—this horribly violent scene. The whole area was ringed with SS. Dogs barked. Machine guns. They knew something was seriously amiss, but none of them had the faintest of notions that in three or four hours they'd be reduced to ashes. When they reached the 'undressing room,' they saw that it looked like an International Information Center! And to the left, at a right angle, was the gas chamber with its massive door. With five or six canisters of gas they could kill around two thousand people. The gas took about ten to fifteen minutes to kill."

(Filip Muller is a survivor of Auschwitz.)

Song: Kadish

(Words by Z. Segalovitch, a Yiddish poet from Vilna; music by Ben Yomen, an American Jewish composer.)

Vifl zaynen shoyn nito.
Zol geheylikt zayn di sho.
Mir baveynen zey on rash,
—Yisgadal veyiskadash...

Vos farblibn iz undz mer,
Vi di durkhgeglite trer
Af di kvorim, af dem ash.
—Yisgadal veyiskadash...

Many are no longer here,
Holy by the hour dear,
We now mourn them all alas,
—Yisgadal veyiskadash...

What for us has then remained,
Only futile tears sustained
Of our dead and tragic ash.
—Yisgadal veyiskadash...

RESISTANCE

Spiritual Resistance

Abraham Foxman, Vilna: Education

(Abraham Foxman was born in Poland in 1940. During the occupation he was on the Aryan side in Vilna. He was brought to America in 1950.)

"The greater part of the resistance was of a passive nature. Attempting to stay alive was passive resistance. Escaping, hiding, or giving birth to a child in the ghetto was resistance. Praying in a congregation , singing, or studying the Bible was resistance. During the first year of the ghetto more than twenty educational units were established, which encompassed more than 80% of the children of school age."

Chaim Kaplan, Warsaw: Simchat Torah

(Chaim Kaplan kept a detailed diary of the Warsaw Ghetto uprising. This is the entry for October 25, 1940. He perished at Treblinka.)

"In the midst of sorrow the holiday of joy. This is not a secular joy, but a 'rejoicing of the Torah,' the same Torah for which we are murdered all day. This was not a raucous celebration but an inner one, a heartfelt joy. Everywhere holiday celebrations were organized, and everywhere prayer groups said the wine blessing."

Ghetto Resistance

Zionist Organizations, Vilna: Call To Action

On January 1, 1942 the first call to resistance was made: "Let us not be led like sheep to the slaughterhouse! Jewish youth: do not believe those that are trying to deceive you. Out of 80,000 Jews of Vilna, only 12,000 are left. Before our own eyes, our parents, our brothers and sisters were taken away. Where are they, those hundreds of men abducted and taken to forced labor by the Lithuanians? Where are the naked men, women, and children who were taken out in that night of terror? Those who are taken out of the gate of the ghetto will never return. Let us not be led like sheep to the slaughter. True, we are weak and helpless, but the only response to the murdered is self-defense. Brethren, it is better to die fighting, like free fighting men than to live at the mercy of the murderers: To defend oneself to the last breath. Take courage!"

Freedom Fighters, Vilna: Battles

"On September 1, 1943, the ghetto was sealed off. The F.P.O. (United Partisan Organization) fighters took up their positions. They set up barricades in two places, one at No. 6 Spitalna Street and the second at No. 12 Strashun Street. The first position was surrounded by the enemy, and because of a lack of ammunition most of the fighters were captured. As the Germans approached the barricade, Jechiel Sheinboim, who was in command, began to fire. The Germans opened with a barrage and blew up the house. Sheinboim and several other fighters lost their lives defending their positions.

"On the 15th of September, the ghetto was again surrounded. The Germans had come with the intention of taking the rest of the Jews for deportation, but when they learned that the ghetto fighters were mobilized to fight, they withdrew from the ghetto.

"On September 23, 1943, (they) ordered the Jews to be ready for evacuation by 12 A.M. The ghetto was then officially to be closed."

(Abraham Foxman)

Bernard Goldstein, Warsaw: A Baby's Life

(Bernard Goldstein was one of the leaders of the General Socialist Labor Organization—the Bund. He joined the underground and survived the destruction of the Warsaw ghetto.)

"Just imagine Chanele, a ghetto fighter, herself but a young child, in a dark cellar suffused with pain, starved and thirsty, awaiting the birth of a baby that would be named for its own father, who had lost his life in battle. Six days after the birth of the child, the uprising was quelled, and three days later everyone had to flee to Prushkow. Chanele was extremely weak; her infant could hardly breathe. The Germans would surely kill them. I made my decision: I would throttle the baby and take Chanele to a bunker. I held the week-old child in my arms. What does one do! One squeeze and we'll be rid of him. However, I didn't have the strength to do it: I hesitated; my fingers faltered. It was as if the infant's father had emerged from his unknown grave. He seemed to live again in his child. I asked several Jews to look after her. Afterward Chanele managed to place the child with a farmer. After the liberation, they lived in Lodz, where I visited them. I held the boy in my arms; I kissed him and wept. Only then did I tell his mother how I had weighed Gabriel's fate at birth."

Song: Es Brent
Our Town is Burning

(Words and music: M. Gebirtig. Written shortly before WWII, this song is a call to Jews to prepare for a last stand in defense of their lives and homes. It became a hymn of the ghetto fighters.)

S'brent! Briderlekh, s'brent!
Oy, undzer orem shtetl nebekh brent!
Beyze vintn mit yirgozn
Raysn, brekhn un tseblozn
Shtarker nokh di vilde flamen,
Alts arum shoyn brent.

> Un ir shteyt un kukt azoy zikh
> Mit farleygte hent
> Un ir shteyt un kukt azoy zich—
> Undzer shtetl brent!

It burns! brothers, it burns!
Our poor shtetl pitifully burns!
Angry wind with rage and curses
Tears and shatters and disperses.
Wild flames leap, they twist and turn,
Everything now burns!

And you stand there looking on
Hands folded, palms upturned,
And you stand there looking on—
Our shtetl burns!

It burns! brothers, it burns!
Help can only come if you return
Love which shtetl once inspired,
Take up arms, put out the fire.
Douse it with your blood—be true—
Show what you can do!

Don't just stand there looking on
Hands folded, palms upturned,
Don't just stand, put out the fire—
Our shtetl burns!

Death Camp Rebellion and Sabotage

From Vilna Went Forth Still Another Decree

(Unknown poet)

So out of the camp the young victims
were ushered one after the other,
and into the cars they were thrust with
dispatch—
like cattle, were sealed in together.

The train chugged along without hurry,
it hooted; the sirens kept screeching.
At a station called Pogar it ground to a halt,
and next came the sound of unhitching....

They say in an instant: they'd all been
deceived,
it was to their death they'd been taken!

They broke down the doors of the boxcars,
and tried to snatch at some way of escaping.

They hurled themselves fiercely against the
Gestapo
and tore the brown shirt from his body.

Not far from the martyred, there also lay dead
some
storm troopers, bitten and bloody.

Helen Prus: Should We Try To Escape

(Helen Prus survived Bergen Belsen and now lives
in the United States.)

"We always planned how to escape from the
labor camp. They picked women in the
morning and we used to march to work. There
was one SS man in front and one in the back. If
you were brave enough you could escape, but
where would you escape? Two girls escaped
and they brought them back and they hung
them there for everyone to see. They called us
all up and we stood at attention. They hung
the girls and we all had to watch. When you
saw this who wanted to be hanged. They
scared us with these tactics.

"In the morning they called you out and they
counted you. If someone was missing we all
were punished. We had to stand for two hours
without shoes in the snow shivering in
January."

Attacking The SS

(Olga Lengyel)

"One day a selectee wrested a revolver from an
SS and started to beat him with it. Desperate
courage certainly inspired this gesture, but it
had no effect except to bring mass reprisals.
The Germans held us all guilty; 'collective
responsibility' they called it."

Uprising at Treblinka

(Samuel Rajzman)

"There was a conspiritorial committee whose
task was to avenge at least to some extent the
millions of innocent people executed. They
dreamed of setting fire to the whole camp.
Finally it was decided to get ammunition and
arms from the camp's arsenal.

"On August 2, 1943, while a large group of
masons were working nearby, we managed to

open it. Thus we were able to get one of our comrades into the building and lock him up there. Outside the arsenal there was a pile of debris and bricks. A cart driven by a member of our group drove up to the building ostensibly to remove the debris. Under it, twenty hand grenades, twenty rifles, and several revolvers with cartridges were loaded.

"At 3:45 P.M. we heard the signal—a rifle shot near the gates of the Jewish barracks. This was followed by the detonations of hand grenades. An enormous fire broke out in the whole camp. The arsenal exploded and everything was burned except the 'bath' cabins. Of the 700 workers on the camp grounds, only 150 to 200 succeeded in escaping; the others perished in the camp as well as more than 20 Germans. Of the 150 to 200 who managed to escape, only 12 are still alive; the others were later murdered by the German hangmen."

Buchenwald: Inmates Capture SS Troops

(Corporal Irving Adler was an American soldier who entered the concentration camp a few days after liberation. This is part of a letter to his parents, April 17, 1945.)

"We met a Russian Jew (who was) once a soldier. He was part of the capture of 250 SS men. As the American Army approached, the Germans began to kill and evacuate the prisioners. Finally things started to get hot and they were looking to evacuate themselves. They wired up the entire camp, ready to blow them (the prisioners) all to bits. Suddenly some of them found new energy (the prisoners, that is) and knowing they were to be killed anyway, figured they'd go down fighting. They had some arms hidden but never could get to using them for any good. They shot a few (SS troops) and captured 250 of them just as the Americans arrived. God, how proud they were of that feat. They had the opportunity to kill them all but didn't and when we asked why, he answered what I thought worthy of historic

notice and a tribute to humanity. 'We could have killed them and God only knows how well they deserved it for all the hell they'd wrought upon the world; but with all that suffering and torture, they still wanted to prove to them that they were men, human beings, and so they let them live.'"

Sabotage

"We worked in an ammunition factory together with Germans, but we wore striped clothes. They gave us responsible work but we couldn't sabotage. The SS were watching closely."

(Helen Prus)

"I worked in the Warsaw Ghetto, in a factory repairing German uniforms. To the extent that I was able, I sabotaged that. In a labor camp I worked on ammunition in another factory; there too, all of us, to the extent that we could, sabotaged that."

(Anonymous survivor)

Partisans

Abraham Lissner: A Jewish Partisan in Paris

(Abraham Lissner was born in Poland and was an organizer of the Jewish Partisan Unit in Paris.)

In April 1942, the leaders of the partisans decided to use a time bomb to attack barracks holding German soldiers.

On November 10, 1942, Marcel Rayman and Nathan Lemberger put a time bomb next to a hotel in Montmor, where many senior German officers stayed. The bomb caused a great deal of damage.

In January 1943 the partisans attacked five German military groups on the streets of Paris during the day.

On February 3, 1943, four men and two women from the Jewish partisans, destroyed an anti-aircraft gun. They also attacked a German military barracks full of solders with hand grenades. Before dawn, the women in this group began to carry the explosives over four miles.

On August 26-27, 1943, the partisans effected the third derailment this month. This was on the Paris-Troy line. In this way they destroyed one locomotive and fourteen carloads of weapons.

On June 6, 1944 the Allied Armies landed on the beaches of Normandy! This encouraged the partisans to increase their efforts.
(Attributed to Abraham Lissner)

Vladka Meed: Women Partisans

(Vladka Meed, a survivor of the Warsaw Ghetto, was an active member of the resistance underground.)

Women played an active role in the partisan movement. Some women were nurses, some fought and some worked in the kitchens. Most young women "were couriers like myself." Their mission was to carry money or documents where they were needed.
(Attributed to Vladka Meed)

Song: Zog Nit Keyn Mol
Song of the Partisans

(Poem by Hirsh Glik (1922-44). Music by Dmitri Pokrass. This song become the hymn of the United Partisan Organization in 1943 and spread to Jewish communities throughout the world.)

Zog nit keyn mol az du geyst dem letstn veg,
Khotsh himlen blayene farshteln bloye teg.

Kumen vet nokh undzer oysgebenkte sho—
Es vet a poyk ton undzer trot-mir zaynen do!

Fun grinem palmenland biz vaysn land
    fun shney,
Mir kumen on mit undzer payn, mit undzer
    vey,
Un vu gefaln, s'iz shprits fun undzer blut,
Shprotsn vet dort undzer gvure, undzer mut.

Never say this is the final road for you,
Though leaden skies above may cover
over days of blue.
As the hour that we longed for is so near,
Our step beats out the message—
    we are here!

From lands so green with palms to lands all white with snow,
We shall be coming with our anguish
    and our woe,
And where a spurt of our blood fell on the earth,
There our courage and our spirit have rebirth.

This song was written with our blood and not with lead,
It's not a little tune that birds sing overhead,
This song a people sang amid collapsing walls,
With grenades in hands they heeded
    to the call.

ABANDONMENT BY THE WORLD

Elie Wiesel: Apathy Of Bystanders

"The victims perished not only because of the killers, but also because of the apathy of the bystanders. Those who perished were victims of Nazism and of society—though to different degrees. What astonished us after the torment, after the tempest, was not that so many killers killed so many victims, but that so few cared about us at all."

(Elie Wiesel survived Auschwitz and Buchenwald where his parents and sister were killed. He has written extensively on the Shoah, and received the Nobel Prize for Peace in 1986. He lives in the United States.)

Callousness and Inaction

"America's response to the Holocaust was the result of action and inaction on the part of many people. In the end, the era's most prominent symbol of humanitarianism turned away from one of history's most compelling challenges.

"Callousness closed the United States as an asylum by tightening immigration procedures, and it influenced Latin American governments to do the same.

"Most American intellectuals were indifferent to the struggle for rescue. Most newspapers printed very little about the Holocaust. American mass- circulation magazines all but ignored the Holocaust.

"Strong currents of anti-Semitism and nativism in American society also diminished the possibilities for a sympathetic response."

(David S. Wyman, an historian, is an advisor to the U.S. Holocaust Memorial Council.)

Many Could Have Been Saved

"What could the American government have achieved if it had really committed itself to rescue? The possibilities were narrowed by the Nazis' determination to wipe out the Jews. War conditions themselves also made the rescue difficult. And by mid-1942, when clear news of the systematic murder reached the West, two million Jews had already been massacred and the killing was going forward at a rapid rate. Most likely, it would not have been possible to rescue millions. But without impeding the war effort, additional tens of thousands— probably hundreds of thousands—could have been saved."

(David S. Wyman)

What Could Have Been Done

"These are a few of the many things that could have been done which would have saved thousands of Jews:

"A campaign to stimulate and assist escapes would have led to a sizable outflow of Jews. Strong pressure needed to be applied to neutral countries near the Axis to take Jews in. Much more effort should have gone into finding ways to send in food and medical supplies.

"The measures taken by Raoul Wallenberg in Budapest should have been implemented by all neutral diplomatic missions and repeated in city after city throughout Axis Europe.

"The Air Force could have eliminated the Auschwitz killing installations.

"Roosevelt, Churchill, and the Pope might have made clear to the Nazis their full awareness of the mass-murder program and their severe condemnation of it."
(David S. Wyman)

Moral Imperative

"There was a moral imperative to attempt everything possible that would not hurt the war effort. If that had been done, even if few or no lives had been saved, the moral obligation would have been fulfilled."
(David S. Wyman)

Apathy

"It was not a lack of workable plans that stood in the way of saving many thousands more European Jews. Nor was it insufficient shipping, the threat of infiltration of subversive agents, or the possibility that rescue projects would hamper the war effort. The real obstacle was the absence of a strong desire to rescue Jews."
(David S. Wyman)

Song: Vu Ahin Zol Ikh Geyn? Where Shall I Go?

(This song is attributed to S. Korntayer who died in the Warsaw Ghetto in 1942. The music is attributed to Oscar Strock. Written before the war, this song was popular in the ghettos and displacement camps.)

Der yid vert geyogt un geplogt—
Nisht-zikher iz far im yeder tog;
Zayn lebn iz a fintstere nakht;
Zayn shtrebn, alts far im iz farmakht.
Farlozn, bloyz mit sonim, keyn fraynd,
Keyn hofenung, on a zikhern haynt.

> Vu ahin zol ikh geyn,
> Ver kon entfern mir?
> Vu ahin zol ikh geyn,
> Az farshlosn z'yede tir?
> S'iz di velt groys genug,
> Nor far mir iz eng un kleyn-
> Vu a blik
> Kh'muz tsurik,
> S'iz tseshtert yede brik;
> Vu ahin zol ikh geyn?

The Jew's always hounded and plagued,
Not sure of his hour or his day.
His life is in darkness enclosed,
His strivings are thwarted, opposed.
Deserted, no friends, only foe,
No safe place, no safe day to know.

> Tell me where shall I go,
> Who can answer my plea?
> Tell me where shall I go,
> Every door is barred to me?
> Though the world's large enough,
> There's no room for me I know,
> What I see
> S'not for me,
> Each road's closed, I'm not free—
> Tell me where shall I go.

RIGHTEOUS GENTILES

Italy

(Ivo Herzer now lives in Virginia.)

"I was sixteen in 1941 when I fled with my parents from the capital of Croatia (Yugoslavia). It was then a fascist state which began a terror against Jews. We were eventually allowed to stay in the Italian zone of occupation.

"Suddenly in November 1942 we were all rounded up and taken to camps. This was a decision taken, from what I can hear or see from the documents, by those in the foreign ministry who were collaborating with the Italian Army on the rescue . They had to stave off the constant German pressure for the extradition of the Jews.

"The camp commandant assured us that as long as the Italian flag was there, we would be assured that nothing untoward would happen. We organized the camp into a real community. The Italian Army even let us build a hut for our religious services. We had schools, and the army even gave us textbooks. The Italians understood not only that they should not kill us, but that we were in need of recognition as human beings, so they gave us a temple and a school."

Denmark

(Leo Goldberger who is now a Professor of Psychology in New York, came to Denmark from Czechoslovakia in 1934 with his family when his father took up the post of Chief Cantor of the Great Synagogue in Copenhagen.)

"The warning that the Germans were planning to round us all up and send us off to a concentration camp came near the end of September from a courageous German in the high command's office in Copenhagen—naval counselor G.F. Duckwitz. It was forwarded to us through Danish intermediaries and announced a few days prior to Rosh Hashanah in the Synagogue.

"The money (for passage on a fishing boat) was forthcoming from a pastor, Henry Rasmussen. (I should add that Pastor Rasmussen refused repayment after the war.)

"The following night we were standing, huddled in some low bushes along the beach. Then finally the lights flashed. We walked straight into the sea. We were hauled aboard the boat, directed in whispers to lie concealed in the cargo area, there to stretch out covered by smelly canvasses; in the event the German patrols were to inspect the boat, we would be passed over as fish. There seemed to have been some 20 other Jews aboard. A few hours later, bright lights and the pastoral scenery of Skane along the coast of Sweden appeared.

"There were thousands of others all across Denmark helping and caring, tending to us—some 7,200 of us as it turned out. What a magnificent feat!"

Chambon-sur-Lignon, France

(Hanne Liebmann now lives in the United States.)

"Originally there were seven of us young people who came from the concentration camp in Gurs. In the camp, we were asked whether we would like to leave and go to a French village. We were not given a lot of information, other than that there were people who wanted to take youngsters out of the camp, that they wanted to help us, that there was a Protestant pastor (André Trochmé) involved, and that the community at large supported him in his effort. I said, 'Yes, I want to leave,' and that was that.

"We came to Le Chambon, the seven of us, and we were received very wonderfully. We were placed in a home where there were about 20-25 boys and girls from outside of France, some French Jewish children, and some non-Jewish children—all sorts of children. We really found a haven there.

"Then in 1942, things became more dangerous, and we had to be hidden. We were taken to farms and the farmers took us without a question. They were happy to have us, and they shared their bread with us, though there was very little of that. I can say that I think my faith in human kind—perhaps this is true for all of us—was really reestablished by those gentle people."

Cracow, Poland

(Carola Sapetowa, a Polish woman.)

"I (Carola Sapetowa, a Polish woman who worked for a Jewish family) became separated from the family when all Jews were segregated into the ghetto. In March 1943, the ghetto was liquidated. The youngest chanced to stay with me. On that day I approached the gate of the ghetto, and it was surrounded by SS men and Ukrainians. People ran about, woebegone. Suddenly I caught sight of the mother. She saw me too, and whispered to Saliusha, the little girl, 'Go to Carolcha.' Without wasting a moment, she glided miraculously through the heavy, high boots of the Ukrainians and ran toward me with outstretched arms.

"The local community knew I was hiding Jewish children, and I was threatened and hounded from all sides. Everyone insisted that I hand the children over to the Gestapo—otherwise, the village would be ravaged and burned, and its people would be killed.

"A novel thought occurred to me. I seated the children in a wagon and, as I drove through the village, assured the peasants that I was going to drown them. They believed me. At night I brought the children back and hid them in a neighbor's loft.

"After that things calmed down until the Red Army arrived."

Holland

(Marion P. van Binsbergen Pritchard was honored by Yad Vashem in 1983 for helping Jews during the occupation. She now lives in Vermont.)

"I was asked by two men in the Dutch Resistance Movement, to find a place for a man with three small children, aged four, two and two weeks. I moved out into part of a large house in the country. Friends helped take up the floorboards under the rug and build a hiding place in case of raids. These did occur with increasing frequency, and one night we had a very narrow escape.

"The Germans, accompanied by a Dutch Nazi policeman, came and searched the house. They did not find the hiding place, but they had learned from experience that sometimes it paid to go back to a house they had already searched, because by then the hidden Jews might have come out of the hiding place. The baby had started to cry so I let the children out. Then the Dutch policeman came back alone. I had a small revolver that a friend had given me, but I had never planned to use it. I felt I had no choice except to kill him.

LIBERATION

Primo Levi: Germans Leave—Russians Arrive

January 18. "The Germans were no longer there. The towers were empty."

January 19. Decay of the Camp. "We went out into the wind of a freezing day of fog, poorly wrapped up in blankets. What we saw resembled nothing that I had ever seen or heard described. The Lager, hardly dead, had already begun to decompose. No more water or electricity, broken windows and doors slamming to in the wind, loose iron-sheets from the roofs screeching, ashes from the fire drifting high, afar. Ragged, decrepit, skeleton-like patients at all able to move dragged themselves everywhere over the frozen soil.

"They had ransacked all the empty huts in search of food and wood; no longer in control of their own bowels, they had fouled everywhere, polluting the precious snow, the only source of water remaining in the whole camp."

Regaining Humanity. "Towarowski proposed to the others that each of them offer a slice of bread to us three. It was the first human gesture that occurred among us. I believe that that moment can be dated as the beginning of the change by which we who had not died, slowly changed from Haftlinge (prisoners) to men again."

January 22. "By now there were beds in all the huts occupied by corpses as rigid as wood, whom nobody troubled to remove. The ground was too frozen to dig graves; many bodies were piled up in a trench."

January 24. "*Liberty.* The breach in the barbed wire gave us a concrete image of it. To anyone who stopped to think, it signified no more Germans, no more selections, no work, no blows, no roll calls, and perhaps, later, the return. But we had to make an effort to convince ourselves of it, and no one had time to enjoy the thought. All around lay destruction and death."

January 27. The Russians Arrived. "There were four young soldiers on horseback. When they reached the barbed wire, they stopped to look, exchanging a few timid words, and throwing strangely embarrassed glances at the sprawling bodies, at the battered huts and at the few still alive.

"They did not greet us, nor did they smile; they seemed oppressed not only by compassion but by a confused restraint which sealed their lips and bound their eyes to the funereal scene. It was that shame we knew so well, the shame that drowned us after the selections, and every time we had to watch or submit to, some outrage: the shame the Germans did not know, that the just man experiences at another man's crime; the feeling of guilt that such a crime should exist, that it should have been introduced irrevocably into the world of things that exist, and that his will for good should have proved too weak or null, and should not have availed in defense."

(Primo Levi was an Italian chemist who survived Auschwitz. After the war he returned to Italy and wrote a number of important books on his experience.)

Eugene Heimler: Forced March Then Freedom

With the Americans advancing from the west, the SS marched prisoners of Buchenwald east to Czechoslovakia. "As soon as we reached the first houses we saw that we had arrived home.

In the center of the village the crowd was lining the pavement like a guard of honor, waving their handkerchiefs at us as though we were returning victorious from the war.

"The SS led us to an evacuated school building; and here the women brought large pots of soup, and we were able to look into their tearful faces with our bellies full for the first time since the beginning of our wandering. Bitterly the women turned toward our SS guards, shaking their clenched fists in the air: `Murderers, you'll pay for this!' The men of the village paraded threateningly around the school. Our guards were terrified, and decided to take us back to German territory. And then we four youngsters went to the latrine, clambered over the fence, and within a few minutes were swallowed up by the forest. We were free—at last."

(Eugene Heimler was taken to Buchenwald after the Nazis overran Hungary in 1944. He survived by escaping on a march in Czechoslovakia.)

American Liberators

Too weak to stand, they lay
on straw under heavy blankets,
skin stretched so taut
over joints they couldn't
bend their arms.
When we passed by they
cowered against the wall,
turned their faces
from the expected blow.

Near the crematoria, I
remember stooping down
and picking up a piece
of something black: I
realized it was a bone.
I was going to throw it
down again. I thought,
My God. This may be all
that's left of someone.
So I wrapped it up in
my handkerchief and
carried it with me. It was

a couple of days later
that I dug it out of my
pocket. And I buried it.

(Anonymous.)

Unbelievable Sight

"I saw today, completely, one of the large concentration camps captured but a few days ago. In general all I can say is that it's unbelievable and even now when I think back of what I saw I don't believe it myself. Truckloads and truckloads of bodies and pieces of bodies, plus ashes and burnt flesh are being removed every day but the place is still cluttered with same.

"A number of those who are still living can still walk and talk but surely a slight wind would knock them over. Most of them are too weak to move from their "bed"—(bed: a shelf with living and dead bodies on top of each other). Their bodies are actual skeletons, just about every bone pushing upon their thin and almost transparent flesh. In every sense of the word they are the living dead."

(Corporal Irving Adler, unpublished letter to his parents, April 17, 1945)

Yiddisha Soldatun Greeted

"There were hundreds of Jews left. As we walked through they lifted their shaven heads upon the two bones that were necks, moaned and groaned but forced a smile for us, stretched out their hands for a cigarette or fruit bars or gum or anything we could spare, clapping their hands in pride at the Yiddisha "soldatun." (They were) all so typically Jewish, freckled face kids, old bald headed men looking like any American Jew from the Bronx and Bronxville. We went part of the way with one 12 year old boy who looked surely like a Brooklyn product. He held our hands as we walked and had a group of his younger friends clammering about us. Everyone there, it seemed, excitedly tried to find some GI to speak to and show around and tell the same story."

(Irving Adler)

SURVIVORS

First Reactions

Primo Levi: Pain in Surviving
(Primo Levi survived Auschwitz.)

"For us even the hour of liberty rang out grave and muffled, and filled our soul with joy and yet with a painful sense of pudency, so that we should have liked to wash our consciences and our memories clean from the foulness that lay upon them.

"In the very hour in which every threat seemed to vanish, in which a hope of a return to life ceased to be crazy, I was overcome—as if a dyke had crumbled—by a new and greater pain, previously buried and relegated to the margins of my consciousness by other more immediate pains: the pain of exile, of my distant home, of loneliness, of friends lost, of youth lost and of the host of corpses all around."

Eugene Heimler: I lost everything
(Eugene Heimler had been in Buchenwald; he survived by escaping on a march in Czechoslovakia.)

(Immediately after liberation) "I began to cry. I fell down on to the deep brown earth and breathed in the smell of the fields, and it was good. I was part of the world and of the present again, and tears had meaning because I had lost everything except my life. I knew that all the people I loved were dead. I knew that the freedom I had gained would be difficult to bear, and that it would be long before I found peace once more."

Nelly Sachs
(Nelly Sachs fled from Germany to Sweden in 1940. She received the Nobel Prize for Literature in 1966)

Chorus of the Rescued

We, the rescued,
From whose hollow bones death had
    begun to whittle his flutes,

And on whose sinews he had already
    stroked his bow—
Our bodies continue to lament
With their mutilated music.
We, the rescued,
The nooses wound for our necks still dangle
before us in the blue air—
Hourglasses still fill with our dripping blood.
We, the rescued,
The worms of fear still feed on us.
Our constellation is buried in dust.
We, the rescued,
Beg you:
Show us your sun, but gradually.
Lead us from star to star, step by step.
Be gentle when you teach us to live again.
Lest the song of a bird,
Or a pail being filled at the well,
Let our badly sealed pain burst forth again
and carry us away—
We beg you:
Do not show us an angry dog, not yet—
It could be, it could be
That we will dissolve into dust—
Dissolve into dust before your eyes.
For what binds our fabric together?
We whose breath vacated us,
Whose soul fled to Him out of that midnight
Long before our bodies were rescued
Into the ark of the moment.

But in the night

But in the night
when dreams pull away
walls and ceiling with a breath of air,
the trek to the dead begins.
You search for them under the stardust—. . .

Thus dawn comes
strewn with the red seed of the sun
and night has cried it self out
into the day—

Abba Kovner

(Abba Kovner was a leader in the resistance in Vilna
and in surrounding forests. He lives in Israel where
he won the Brenner Prize and the Israeli Prize.)

From: What Is Not in the Heart

Useless: I try now to define who you were—
word—shadows! Only your returning shadow
exists. My hands will never touch you. Your
coffin never leaves my shoulders.

From: My Little Sister

In seventy-seven funerals we circled the wall
and the wall stood.
From the promised land I called you,
I searched for you
among heaps of small shoes.
At every approaching holiday.
No man will cure,
no heaven,
the offense of your scalding silence.

As in a flood dammed too late,
they will come, come to the shore,
their hearts full of pity, to help
the survivors with swollen feet
into the book of chronicles,
to extend a brother's hand.
And they gave them a hand
in spite of their ugly smell.
And before heart and mind could separate
they cried,
and applauded them
As in a melodrama that's over:
the CHARACTERS
are asked
to step in front of the curtain.

They came out.
They stretched their whole
hands for the bread
still fearing hunger.

Primo Levi: Return To Death Camps

"I returned to Auschwitz twice, in 1965 and in 1982. I didn't feel much when I visited the central camp. The Polish government has transformed it into a kind of national monument. The huts have been cleaned and painted, trees have been planted and flowerbeds laid out. I did, however, experience a feeling of violent anguish when I entered Birkenau Camp (next to Auschwitz), which I had never seen as a prisoner. Here nothing has changed. (A friend of mine) showed me that from the tiny window you could see the ruins of the cremation furnace. In her day, one saw the flame issuing from the chimney. She had asked the older women: 'What is that fire?' And they replied: 'It is we who are burning.'"

Charlotte Dembo: Giving Birth

"From what I've observed among the numerous camp survivors, there are two categories: those who left and those who are still there. I'm one of the latter. So on September 24, 1952, while I was giving birth, I didn't think of the joy that a child would bring me; I was thinking—and had been for days and months and years—I was thinking of the women of my age who had died in degradation without that joy."

Elie Wiesel: Survivors Are Weary

(Elie Wiesel, who survived Auschwitz, has written extensively on the Shoah, and won the Nobel Prize.)

"First ignored, then resented, we have seen our message distorted, cheapened, trivialized, commercialized so much that we do not know what to do: to speak or not to speak , to give more words or to take them back. For years we have tried to tell the tale, but now we feel more misunderstood than ever. The survivors are weary of whispering, alerting, warning, protesting, compelling others to remember, weary of trying to preserve the sacred dimension of a certain experience, a certain despair, a certain defiance. Oh, yes, we are weary."

Song: A Yeder Ruft Mikh Zhamele
They Call Me Zhamele

(Sung by an eight-year-old boy in an orphan asylum in Lublin in 1945. Author unknown, music by Bernardo Feuer.)

Yeder ruft mikh Zhamele,
Ay, vi mir iz shver.
Kh'hob gehat a memele,
Kh'hob zi shoyn nit mer.
Kh'hob gehat a tatele,
Hot er mikh gehit;
Itst bin ikh a shamatele,
Vayl ikh bin a yid.

Kh'hob gehat a heymele,
Itster iz mir shlekht;
Ikh bin vi a beheymele,
Vos der talyen shekht.
Got, du kuk fun himele,
Af dayn erd arop,
Kuk tsu vi dayn blimele
Rayst der talyen op...

They all call me Zhamele,
Oh, it's hard for me;
 I once had a mother dear,
Who knows where she can be?
I once had a father dear,
His love for me was true,
Now I'm just a little rag
Because I am a Jew.

I once had a little home,
Now I feel despair.
Like a little calf I moan
When slaughtered without care.
God, you look down from the sky
On your earth below,
Have you seen your flowers die,
Cut down by brutal foe?

REBUILDING LIVES

Roni Alshech from Bulgaria, is now Yael Shemtov living in Israel.

"One day at the end of December 1947 a member of the (Zionist) group came to my home and said, 'Tomorrow, we are all leaving for Israel, are you ready to come?' I did not hesitate. I went down the street to look for my mother and told her. As was to be expected, she did not welcome the news. Even in those difficult days it seemed very impetuous and rushed. 'Already, now? With whom? How?' and all the other questions that are so reasonable when a young daughter suddenly announces that she is leaving her home, her family and way of life to go on an unknown road to an unknown country."

Valley of Dry Bones: Ezekiel 37

"The hand of the Lord was upon me. He carried me by the spirit of the Lord and set me down in midst of the valley, and it was full of bones. He said to me, 'Prophesy over these bones and say to them: Dry bones: I will cause breath to enter into you and you shall live.' So I prophesied as I had been commanded. As I prophesied, suddenly there was a noise and a commotion, and the bones came together, bone to matching bone. The breath came into them, they came to life and stood up upon their feet. And He said to me, 'Prophesy, and say to them: Thus said the Lord God: I will open your graves and lift you out, O My people, and I will bring you to the land of Israel.'"

Allegra Korman from Castoria, Greece survived Auschwitz and now lives in Cedarhurst, N.Y.

Greece
"After we were liberated my first instinct was to go back home to seek out any survivors. I found one brother and a cousin. I went to Athens to a Jewish home for girls supported by the National Council of Jewish Women. ORT provided schooling for many of us to learn a trade.

United States

"In December 1948 I came to the United States where a brother I had never met helped me. It was a new struggle to learn how to live in a free world, learn a new language. With very high determination to push back my past experiences and go forward, I went to school to learn the language and America's history. I got married, raised a family and went back to school and received a bachelor's degree.

"I am presently working as an Adjunct Assistant Professor at the Fashion Institute of Technology. I am dedicated to teaching young people the profession of pattern making. I also make appearances at any Hebrew or other schools to speak about the holocaust so that the world will never forget that it really happened."

Trude Noack left Langen, Germany in 1937 and now lives in Port Jefferson, N.Y.

Saying Good-bye

"I came by boat. My father took me to Hamburg. I was a scared, frightened 17 year old child. When the train left my mother held onto the train: I was her only child and to let a child go to America—that was the end of the world. It was terrible. My father took me to Hamburg and when I said good-bye to him it was the last time I saw him."

Arrival in America

"I arrived on Thursday night November 11, 1937. I was met at the pier by a chauffer driven Rolls Royce. My uncle who was very wealthy had reluctantly sent me papers but refused to take any responsibility for me. On Friday morning I was taken to the Council of Jewish Women for a job as a maid. My first job was as a chamber maid and waitress on Park Avenue. The first time I put on the uniform I was crying but I knew it was something I had to do. I had a trousseau for my future which I brought here but I could not bring money out. It included a

maid's uniform for when I was married and I had a maid. Little did I know that I would be the maid. I cried myself to sleep many nights. The first year was awfully lonely. I knew it was temporary and expected my parents would eventually come."

Marriage

"On Rosh Hashanah 1938 I met my first husband. He was a German refugee from the Rhineland. He took a job as a butcher at night. This was the only thing he could get. This was the depression and American-born people couldn't get jobs. I was very lonely; he proposed and I accepted. Neither of us had any money and we had parents in Germany we were saving to get out. We got married in October 1939.

"A year or so later, I came home from work and there was this letter from the Commandant of the camp that my father had died of starvation and malnutrition on December 26, 1940."

Siegmar Silber, born in Leipzig, Germany, was sent to England on the last "kindertransport," in 1939. He now lives in New Jersey.

Leaving Germany

"I do not have any recollection of Germany or my parents. I was born on October 12, 1936 and left my parents toward the end of August, 1939. Until I was four years old, I spoke a mixture of German and English."

Childhood in England

"I lived with two Anglican families. I lived with the Mansfields from the age of 5 to the age of 11- 1/2 and adjusted to a poor, yet loving environment. I attended Cambridgeshire High School for Boys. There, I worked quite hard at my studies. The atmosphere for learning was supportive and stimulating.

"The scouting organization in which I was a leader was identified with the Holy Trinity

Church, and several times a year the scouts would have parades and participate in church services. By comparison, the small, local synagogue seemed pale and lifeless."

Arriving in the United States
"Probably the worst experience in my life was being wrenched out of the environment in Cambridge, which I perceived as comfortable, and being sent to America.

"Against all advice, Meyer (my adoptive father) was determined to have me. Here the mitzvah of saving a Jewish child from falling into the hands of Christians proved to be a motivating factor, especially as Meyer who was born in Lodz had vivid recollections of the late nineteeth century pogroms.

"When I arrived in Paterson (New Jersey), Meyer was 66 and Gussie (my adoptive mother), was 61 years of age. Although they never had children, Meyer had been 'Uncle' to the entire world and children of all ages addressed him as such. In the beginning, Meyer showed me off very much as his contemporaries showed off their grandchildren. Gussie had no part in these exercises; in fact, she was peeved at my having taken center stage.

College, Career and Marriage
"I went to MIT where I studied biochemical engineering. In my junior year, I took off a year and worked, then transferred to Columbia University where I studied history and English. I worked as a high school teacher for a while, earned a Master's degree from Yeshiva University and later went to Fordham Law school at night. I am now a patent attorney.

"One impact the holocaust had was to make me realize that I needed to form a family as soon as I could. I needed to replace the loss. At twenty-one I was married and at twenty-five our first child was born."

Harry and Helen Prus from Stashov and Kroszniewice, Poland, survived concentration camps and now live in Stony Brook, NY.

Bergen Belsen DP Camp,
"The English were good to us; they took care of us. We spent four years in the DP camp. We met through a cousin, and we got married in Bergen Belsen in 1946. When they told me I was going to have twins I was so scared. I was young and we didn't know where we were going."

Journey to America
"The trip was horrible. They kept us in Bremen for weeks and weeks. We came on a military boat. The men were downstairs where the soldiers used to be and upstairs they kept the women and children. My kids were sick the whole time. Some kids got measels and died and they threw them in the ocean. When you see things like that you get scared. It was hell. The crossing was 12 days but it seemed like a lifetime."

Starting in America
"When we came to N.Y. it was very hard. The Joint Distribution Committee helped us. Later they sent us to Camden, N.J. We didn't know how to speak English. We met a man who told us that if you want to be independent, learn upholstery so you can open your own store. I got a job to learn upholstery."

Accomplishments
"I tell you one thing, we did good in this country. We opened up an upholstery business in Brooklyn. It was a beautiful business and we had a beautiful house. Our kids went to yeshiva. We kept all the traditions. Our daughter went to Brooklyn College and later got a Ph.D. She is now a school administrator. Our son went to Polytechnic Institute for engineering. Our other daughter is an accountant. Look what we accomplished. After all, we are strangers in the land, but we tried our best and we raised a good family. It was

very hard. We both worked very hard. We put everything into our children. But we still have very terrible nightmares."

Marika Frank Abrams from Debrecin, Hungary, survived Auschwitz and Bergen-Belsen, and came to the United States in 1948 with a scholarship to the University of Washington arranged by the Hillel Foundation. She lives in Seattle, Washington.

University
"Being here seemed such a dream, so unreal, so unbelievable. And the Hillel scholarship offered us everything. The Jewish sorority paid for our room and board. It was all very mysterious because we didn't know what a sorority was."

Jews Unaware
"The sorority girls were nice girls but we had nothing to talk about to each other. They were not at all aware of what the war meant to the Jewish people. I don't blame them. Their parents were no better. Once I was invited for a weekend by a girl who was the president of the sorority house. Her father told me that the Jews of his town had a very hard time during the war. A window was even broken in the synagogue. He was perfectly serious and I was just speechless."

Careers
"After I got my Art School degree I found I could be quite succesful as a painter, but not make enough money to live on. I was represented by the best gallery in the Northwest but it was not a dependable way to make a living. Ten years after I left school I went back to do a master's degree in library science, and while doing that I was engaged in designing sets for two operas."

Marriage
"My husband, Sid Abrams, was one of the three Seattle boys who went to Europe to help bring immigrants to Palestine, and were involved in Aliyah Bet activities in Bulgaria, Italy and France."

Satisfactions
"I can look back on moments of great pleasure. In 1953, just after my son Eddie was born, I became an American citizen. I can remember that I had just learned to drive and I drove around with the baby in the the car, being an American citizen. I felt like the queen of the world!"

Sadness
"A kind of sadness, however, never leaves me. I didn't know that others could see it until my son, only five or six years old, asked me once, 'Mommy, why is your smile so sad?' And I realized that he divined my real feelings. I was always sad."

As a Witness
"I have a close friend, very social conscious, very responsible, always wanting to do the right thing. When I tried to talk about the Holocaust, my friend said, 'Don't talk about it. I don't want to hear it. I love you but I don't want to hear it.' And I thought to myself, 'How could you possibly love me if you don't want to hear? You don't know what love is.'"

Israel
"I love Israel. I am very uncritical. I'm too old and tired to live there but I love it with all my heart. If I couldn't have come to America I would have gone to Israel. But once here I liked it so much I stayed."

IMPLICATIONS FOR OUR TIME

Jewish Continuity

Emil Fackenheim: The 614th Commandment

(Emil Fackenheim, born in Germany, was ordained in Berlin. In 1940 he made his way to Canada where he served as a rabbi and professor.)

"There emerges what I will boldly term a 614th commandment: *the authentic Jew of today is forbidden to hand Hitler yet another posthumous victory.* If the 614th commandment is binding upon the authentic Jew then we are first commanded to survive as Jews, lest the Jewish people perish. We are commanded, second, to remember in our very guts and bones the martyrs of the Holocaust, lest their memory perish. We are forbidden, thirdly, to deny or despair of God, however much we may have to contend with Him, or with belief in Him, lest Judaism perish. We are forbidden, finally, to despair of the world as the place which is to become the kingdom of God, lest we help make it a meaningless place in which God is dead or irrelevant and everything is permitted. To abandon any of these imperatives, in response to Hitler's victory at Auschwitz, would be to hand him yet other, posthumous victories."

Elie Wiesel: Birth of His Son

(Elie Wiesel was born in Sighet, Rumania. He survived Birkenau, Auschwitz, Buna and Buchenwald. After the war he lived in Paris and later came to the United States. He was awarded the Nobel Prize.)

After the birth of his son, Wiesel said: "It is really the Jew in me that says that we must go on, we must build endurance, no matter what. We must show that although there is no hope, we must invent hope."

Abe Weiss: Become Them

(Abe Weiss is a survivor of the Shoah who now lives in Israel.)

"Questions and Answers"

The Holocaust left its mark on each
 surviving Jew,
There and everywhere.
Why Them and not us?
Were they the sinners and we so righteous?
Did we do enough?
How much did we know?
Was there a lesson learned?
The same baseless hatred remains.
Could it happen again?...
Not while there is an Israel.
How do we replace Them?
By becoming Them.

God

Martin Buber: The Hidden God

(Buber was born in Vienna in 1878. He left Germany in 1938 and went to Palestine where he became a professor at the Hebrew University.)

"The estrangement (from God) has become too cruel, the hiddenness too deep. One can still 'believe' in the God who allowed those things to happen, but can one still speak to Him? Can one still hear His word? Dare we recommend to the survivors of Auschwitz, the Job of the gas chambers: 'Give thanks unto the Lord, for He is good; for His mercy endureth forever?' Do we stand overcome before the hidden face of God like the tragic hero of the Greeks before faceless fate? No, rather even now we contend, we too, with God. We do not put up with earthly being; we struggle for its redemption, and struggling we appeal to the help of our Lord, who is again and still a hiding one."

I believe in God...

I believe in the sun even when it is not shining.
I believe in love even when feeling it not.
I believe in God even when He is silent.

(Inscription on walls where Jews hid from Nazis.)

Elie Wiesel

Mystery
"Perhaps some day someone will explain how, on the level of man, Auschwitz was possible; but on the level of God, it will forever remain the most disturbing of mysteries."

Madness of Belief
"One has to be mad today to believe in God and in man—one has to be mad to believe. One has to be mad to want to remain human."

"At Auschwitz not only man died, but also the idea of man. It was its own heart the world incinerated at Auschwitz."

God Shares Suffering
In *Gates of the Forest*, by Elie Wiesel, Elijah says to Gavriel: "You think you're cursing Him, but your curse is praise; you think you're fighting Him, but all you do is open yourself to Him; you think you're crying out your hatred and rebellion, but all you're doing is telling Him how much you need His support and forgiveness. No, you mustn't blaspheme against someone who shares your suffering."

Midrash: God Shares Israel's Suffering

"God called to him (Moses) out of the thornbush."
(Exodus 3.4)

The Holy One praised be He, said to Moses: "Do you not feel that I am in pain just as Israel is in pain? Understand this from the place out of which I am speaking to you: the thorns! If one could possibly say so, I am sharing Israel's sufferings."

That is the reason why it is said in Isaiah 63.9: "In all their afflictions He was afflicted."
(Exodus Rabbah II.5)

Werner Weinberg:
Explanations in Bergen Belsen

(Weinberg survived Bergen Belsen and now lives in the U.S.)

"The question of religious faith in the camp (came) in one of two forms. One was resignation: if He has decreed that I be among the dead of this place, so be it. The other was that God will hear my prayer and save me alive from this hell. The former was defeatest, actually inviting death. The second attitude, the faith of an individual that God would spare his or her life, appeared to be as an expression of egotism and arrogance.

"The God who permitted the unspeakable cruelties, especially those perpetrated on children, could not be 'good' in the accepted sense of the word.

"Our theology became so basic that we made absurd distinctions. For instance: the fact that we were made to stand on punitive roll-call for many hours—that was SS cruelty. But that it was also cold and wet and windy to sharpen our pain—that was God's doing. We were victims not only of human beings' inhumanity—but also of God's ungodliness."

Rabbi Israel Spira: Faith in Redemption

During a makeshift Passover seder in Bergen Belsen Rabbi Spira said, "We who are witnessing the darkest night in history, the lowest moment of civilization, will also witness the great light of redemption, for before the great light there will be a long night, as was promised by our Prophets: 'The people that walked in darkness have seen a great light; they that dwelt in the land of the shadow of death, upon them hath the light shined.' It was to us, my dear children, that our prophets have spoken, to us who dwell in the shadow of death, to us who will live to witness the great light of redemption."

The Task of Humanity Today
Terence Des Pres:
Shoah Defines Our Age

"After Auschwitz, nothing seems stable or unstained—not the values we live by, not our sense of self-worth, not existence itself. The Holocaust has forced upon us a radical rethinking of everything we are and do.

"Every age produces the event which defines it, and in our time the Holocaust is ours. It demands that we face the kind of limitless horror our technological and bureaucratic civilization makes possible. The exterminating angel has arisen before us, blocking all light, demanding battle in a night without promise of dawn."

Elie Wiesel:
Invent Reason, Create Beauty

"This is what I think we are trying to prove to ourselves, desperately, because it is desperately needed: in a world of absurdity, we must invent reason; we must create beauty out of nothingness. And because there is murder in this world—and we are the first ones to know it—and we know how hopeless our battle may appear, we have to fight murder and absurdity, and give meaning to the battle, if not to our hope."

Rudy Appel

(Born in Mannheim, Germany he fled to France after Kristallnacht in 1938, and was protected by the people of Le Chambon. He now lives in the U.S. and has been active in the effort to rescue Soviet Jews.)

Indifference to Suffering
"Many non-Jews didn't act because they

thought that as long as it isn't their family who is in danger, the attacks have nothing to do with them. And it is my perception that not even all Jews helped one another. The same applies today. How indifferent we are when we hear about the suffering and oppression of others. Elie Wiesel has said that evil can only flourish when decent people do nothing. If it's not our own skin, we don't usually get too excited."

Our Self-righteousness

"We should not feel so self-righteous when we complain about how others did not help. A survivor I know lost her entire family and speaks about how non-Jews did not help her relatives. People who know her well, tell me that she is very protective of her surviving family. They doubt she would have been willing to take the risks for others she expected them to take for her. Also, we Jews complain about anti-semitism and yet some of us harbor prejudices of our own."

Abraham Joshua Heschel:
God Awaits Us

(In 1938 Heschel was expelled from Germany to Poland along with other Polish Jews. He later went to England. In 1940 he came to the U.S. where he taught at Hebrew Union College-Jewish Institute of Religion and later (1945) at the Jewish Theological Seminary.)

"At no time has the earth been so soaked with blood. The vision of the sacred has all but died in the soul of man. There is a divine dream which the prophets and rabbis have cherished and which fills our prayers, and permeates the acts of true piety. It is the efforts of man, by his dedication to the task of establishing the kingship of God in the world. God is waiting for us to redeem the world. We should not spend our life hunting for trivial satisfactions while God is waiting constantly and keenly for our effort and devotion. The Almighty has not created the universe that we may have opportunities to satisfy our greed, envy and ambition. We have not survived that we may waste our years in vulgar vanities. The martyrdom of millions demands that we consecrate ourselves to the fulfillment of God's dream of salvation."

Ruth Minsky Sender:
Remember! Never Again!

(Ruth Sender survived Auschwitz and now lives in Commack, N.Y.)

"As a holocaust survivor I carry a heavy burden, the burden of remembering, and a painful duty, the duty of passing on those memories so the world would learn and it should never happen again. I, the survivor make you, today, witnesses. Together we take on the painful duty of remembering, of standing guard against indifference, against prejudice, against injustice."

Prayer After Readings

O God, give us ears to hear and hearts to
understand the memories these words bring,
so that we might acknowledge
their lives and their suffering,
their death and their resistance,
their survival, their despair and their hopes.

Praised are You, for memory and words,
for hearts that speak and hearts that listen.

* *

ALEINU

* *

YIZKOR

* *

Aleinu

All Rise

עָלֵֽינוּ לְשַׁבֵּֽחַ לַאֲדוֹן הַכֹּל, לָתֵת גְּדֻלָּה
לְיוֹצֵר בְּרֵאשִׁית, שֶׁלֹּא עָשָֽׂנוּ כְּגוֹיֵי
הָאֲרָצוֹת, וְלֹא שָׂמָֽנוּ כְּמִשְׁפְּחוֹת הָאֲדָמָה;
שֶׁלֹּא שָׂם חֶלְקֵֽנוּ כָּהֶם, וְגֹרָלֵֽנוּ
כְּכָל־הֲמוֹנָם.

We praise the Ruler of all life;
we give glory to our Creator.
Our heritage is ancient and rich;
our role on earth has been unique.
It is our destiny to declare Your unity,
our privilege to proclaim Your sovereignty.

וַאֲנַֽחְנוּ כּוֹרְעִים וּמִשְׁתַּחֲוִים וּמוֹדִים
לִפְנֵי מֶֽלֶךְ מַלְכֵי הַמְּלָכִים, הַקָּדוֹשׁ בָּרוּךְ
הוּא.

We bow before the Sovereign of all rulers, the
Holy One, who alone is to be praised.

All Are Seated

In the anguish of the Shoah
and in the deliverance of a remnant
we seek You, our God.

In light and in darkness
we affirm that You are our Creator,
the One who walks with our people through history,
the One with whom we walk through our own lives.

You are the One in whom we place our trust
that you will remember the hopes of the slain
by redeeming Your shattered world.

You are the One in whom we place our trust
that in spite of everything which strangles hope,
You will help us to continue the sustaining song of
their lives.

You are the One who strengthens our efforts
to bring peace and justice to the world.

You are the One who strengthens our resolve
to keep our people alive.

וְנֶאֱמַר: "וְהָיָה יְיָ לְמֶֽלֶךְ עַל־כָּל־הָאָֽרֶץ;
בַּיּוֹם הַהוּא יִהְיֶה יְיָ אֶחָד וּשְׁמוֹ אֶחָד."

And it is said, "And Adonai will reign over the
earth, on that day Adonai will be One and the
Divine Name, One."

Yizkor

Adonai our Creator,
"Remember the chimneys, the ingenious
     habitations of death
where part of Israel's body drifted as smoke
     through the air."
     (Nelly Sachs)

Remember the mutilated music of their lives.

We lament in fields of loneliness
for six million of our number torn away.

Remember them.

There are some who have no memorial.
They are perished as though they had never
     been.

Forget them not.

Remember the landscape of screams
engraved at entrance gates to death.

Remember the unborn dreams.

Remember the terror of children, whose tears
were burned.

*Remember the agony of parents, whose blessings
were consumed.*

Remember the prayers of the dying
the shame and the suffering of the innocent.

Song: Unter Di Khurves Fun Poyln
Under the Ruins of Poland
     (Poem: Itsik Manger. Music: S. Beresovsky.)

Unter di khurves fun poyln
A kop mit blond hor —

Der kop un say der khurbn
Beyde zenen vor.

    Dolye, mayne dolye.

Iber di khurves fun poyln
Falt un falt der shney,
Der blonder kop fun mayn meydl
Tut mir mesukn vey.

Der veytik zitst baym shraybtish
Un shraybt a langn briv,
Di trer in zayne oygn,
Iz emesdik un tif.

Iber di khurves fun poyln
Flatert a foygl um
A groyser shive-foygl,
Er tsitert mit di fligl frum.

Der groyser shive-foygl
(Mayn dershlogn gemit),
Er trogt oyf zayne fligl
Dos dozike troyer-lid.

Under the ruins of Poland lies a head with blond hair. Both the head and the ruins are true. The snow keeps falling over the ruins of Poland. My head aches for my girl's blond head. Pain is sitting at the desk, writing a long letter. The tears in her eyes are deep and true. A large bird of mourning flutters its wings and bears this song of mourning.

          *   *

O God of Israel, we remember the countless numbers of our people who have suffered unspeakable agonies and death. Some were silent sufferers, some rebelled, all were murdered. Some are still remembered by friends and loved ones, others have vanished with no earthly remembrance. We plead that You will remember all of them, that you will hold them in Your heart, that they will find their peace with You.

Reading of Names.

Some communities may wish to read the names of some of those who persished in the Shoah.

Silent Remembrance

Read one or more of the following:

...silence is where the victims dwell...
(Nelly Sachs)

          *   *

We dead of Israel say to you:
We are moving past one more star
Into our hidden God.
(Nelly Sachs)

          *   *

When Rabbi Meir died, there were no more makers of parables. When Ben Zoma died, there were no more expounders. When Rabbi Joshua died, goodness departed from this world.
(Mishnah Sota IX)

When Kalman the shoemaker died, there were no more craftsmen. When Berl the musician died, artistry departed from the world. When Jonah the wagon driver went up in smoke, the roads washed away and troubles grew. When Avreml the orphan died, goodness departed from this world.
(David Roskies)

All Rise

אֵל מָלֵא רַחֲמִים, שׁוֹכֵן בַּמְּרוֹמִים,
הַמְצֵא מְנוּחָה נְכוֹנָה תַּחַת כַּנְפֵי הַשְּׁכִינָה
בְּמַעֲלוֹת קְדוֹשִׁים וּטְהוֹרִים כְּזֹהַר הָרָקִיעַ
מַזְהִירִים, אֶת־נִשְׁמוֹת כָּל־אַחֵינוּ בְּנֵי
יִשְׂרָאֵל, אֲנָשִׁים נָשִׁים וָטַף, שֶׁנִּשְׁחֲטוּ
וְשֶׁנִּשְׂרְפוּ וְשֶׁנֶּהֶרְגוּ, עַל קִדּוּשׁ הַשֵּׁם. אָנָּא
בַּעַל הָרַחֲמִים, הַסְתִּירֵם בְּסֵתֶר כְּנָפֶיךָ
לְעוֹלָמִים וּצְרֹר בִּצְרוֹר הַחַיִּים
אֶת־נִשְׁמוֹתֵיהֶם. יְיָ הוּא נַחֲלָתָם, וְיָנוּחוּ
בְּשָׁלוֹם עַל מִשְׁכְּבוֹתֵיהֶם. וְנֹאמַר אָמֵן.

God full of compassion grant perfect peace in Your sheltering Presence among the holy and the pure, to the souls of the men, women and children of the House of Israel, who were slaughtered and burned in the ghettos and concentration camps of the Shoah. May their memory endure from generation to generation for all time. Master of mercies keep them under Your protecting care in the shadow of Your wings. May they find the peace denied them in this world. May their souls be bound up in the bonds of eternal life. Adonai is now their inheritance. May they rest in peace. And let us say, *Amen.*

Kaddish

יִתְגַּדַּל וְיִתְקַדַּשׁ שְׁמֵהּ רַבָּא בְּעָלְמָא
דִּי־בְרָא כִרְעוּתֵהּ, וְיַמְלִיךְ מַלְכוּתֵהּ
בְּחַיֵּיכוֹן וּבְיוֹמֵיכוֹן וּבְחַיֵּי דְכָל־בֵּית
יִשְׂרָאֵל, בַּעֲגָלָא וּבִזְמַן קָרִיב וְאִמְרוּ: אָמֵן.

יְהֵא שְׁמֵהּ רַבָּא מְבָרַךְ לְעָלַם וּלְעָלְמֵי
עָלְמַיָּא.
יִתְבָּרַךְ וְיִשְׁתַּבַּח, וְיִתְפָּאַר וְיִתְרוֹמַם
וְיִתְנַשֵּׂא, וְיִתְהַדָּר וְיִתְעַלֶּה וְיִתְהַלָּל שְׁמֵהּ
דְּקוּדְשָׁא בְּרִיךְ הוּא, לְעֵלָּא מִן
כָּל־בִּרְכָתָא וְשִׁירָתָא, תֻּשְׁבְּחָתָא וְנֶחֱמָתָא
דַּאֲמִירָן בְּעָלְמָא, וְאִמְרוּ: אָמֵן.
יְהֵא שְׁלָמָא רַבָּא מִן־שְׁמַיָּא וְחַיִּים
עָלֵינוּ וְעַל־כָּל־יִשְׂרָאֵל, וְאִמְרוּ: אָמֵן.
עֹשֶׂה שָׁלוֹם בִּמְרוֹמָיו, הוּא יַעֲשֶׂה
שָׁלוֹם עָלֵינוּ וְעַל־כָּל־יִשְׂרָאֵל, וְאִמְרוּ: אָמֵן.

Yitgadal v'yitkadash sh'mei raba b'alma di v'ra chir'utei, v'yamlich malchutei b'chayeichon u-v'yomeichon u-v'chayei d'chol beit Yisrael, ba-agala u-vi-z'man kariv, v'imru amen.

Y'hei sh'mei raba m'varach l'alam u-l'almei almaya.

Yitbarach v'yishtabach v'yitpa'ar v'yitromam v'yitnasei, v'yit-hadar v'yit'aleh v'yit-halal sh'mei d'kudsha, b'rich hu l'ela min kol birchata v'shirata, tushb'chata v'nechemata da'amiran b'alma, v'imru amen.

Y'hei sh'lama raba min sh'maya v'chayim aleinu v'al kol Yisrael, v'imru amen.

Oseh shalom bi-m'romav hu ya'aseh shalom aleinu v'al kol yisrael, v'imru amen.

May the God of peace send peace and healing to all who mourn.

All Are Seated

We Are Witnesses

God of our fathers and mothers
our eyes are now witnesses
for the suffering of Israel;
our hearts have been torn
as we mourn for our people.
We will not forget not one single thing
not forget to the last generation
lest we ignore
threats to our people
and all human degradation,
or we've learned nothing,
nothing at all.
(Based on "Vow" by Abraham Shlonsky)

One or more of the following songs may be sung:

Song: Am Yisroel Khay
The Jewish People Live!

(This song was written after the Holocaust and was sung in the displaced persons camps in Europe. The words were written by M. Knapheise who now lives in Argentina. The music is by S. Beresovsky.)

Efnt tir un efnt toyer,
Shoyn genug, genug der troyer,
Mit fonen-flater shpant atsind di fray.
Fun di bunkers, fun di lekher
Shtaygn veln mir alts hekher,
Vayl mir zogn: Am yisroel khay!

Vider oyfgeyn vet dos lebn
Un dermit a tikn gebn
Veln mir dos alts vos iz farbay;
Leygt a tsigl tsu a tsigl,
Iber undz geshpreyt di fligl
Hot der goyrl — Am yisroel khay!

> Es shaynt di zun shoyn vider,
> Durkh trern shaynt dos glik,
> Tsum lebn shvester, brider,
> Mir kern zikh tsurik!

Open door and open portal,
It's enough, let's not be mournful,
With flags unfurled and freedom's torch
    held high.
From the burrow from the bunkers,
Going onward's what we long for,
While proclaiming: "Am Yisroel Khay!"

Once again our lives are thriving,
It's our answer for surviving,
Our response to everthing gone by;
Put a boulder on a boulder,
Placed above us winglike shoulders
Has our future: "Am Yisroel Khay!"

> Again the sunshine's ours,
> Through tears our joy returns,
> To life now sisters, brother,
> Our presence we affirm!

Song: Am Yisrael Chai!
The people of Israel live!

עַם יִשְׂרָאֵל חַי
עוֹד אָבִינוּ חַי.

The people of Israel live!
Our God still lives!

Song: Oseh Shalom
The One Who Creates Peace

עֹשֶׂה שָׁלוֹם בִּמְרוֹמָיו, הוּא יַעֲשֶׂה
שָׁלוֹם עָלֵינוּ וְעַל־כָּל־יִשְׂרָאֵל, וְאִמְרוּ אָמֵן.

May the One who creates peace in the heavens
above, establish peace for us and for all Israel,
and let us say: Amen.

Song: Ani MaAmin

אֲנִי מַאֲמִין בֶּאֱמוּנָה שְׁלֵמָה
בְּבִיאַת הַמָּשִׁיחַ.
וְאַף עַל פִּי שֶׁיִּתְמַהְמֵהַּ,
עִם כָּל זֶה אֲנִי מַאֲמִין,
עִם כָּל זֶה אֲחַכֶּה לוֹ
בְּכָל יוֹם שֶׁיָּבוֹא.

I believe with perfect faith
in the coming of the Messiah,
and despite the long delay
I believe the Messianic time will arrive.
(Moses Maimonides)

Acknowledgements

I have made every effort to determine the holders of copyrights to passages used in this work, and to secure permission to use copyrighted material. I am grateful to all those listed below for permission to use the passages indicated. In future editions I will be pleased to correct any errors or omissions inadvertantly made here.

Artia: "We go used...," p. 14, "The heaviest wheel...," p. 20, "Perhaps of the sun...," p. 33, "There's little to eat ...," p. 36, "The sun has...," p. 53, "How beautiful is the world...," p. 56 from ...*I never saw another butterfly*, edited by Hana Volavkova, Copyright (c) 1978 by Artia, Prague. Published by Artia, Prague for Schocken Books, Inc., N.Y. Used with permission of the State Jewish Museum, Prague.

Bergen Belsen Memorial Press: "May God's name..." from Aaron Zeitlin, "Kaddish," *in Leder fun Churbn un Liber fun Gloybn*, I:140, (c) 1967 Bergen Belsen Association. Used with permission of Bergen Belsen Memorial Press.

Martin Buber: "The estrangement..." and "Do we stand...," pp. 61-2 from Martin Buber, *At The Turning*, Farrar, Straus and Young, Copyright (c) 1952. Reprinted with persmission of the estate of Martin Buber.

B'nai B'rith Hillel Foundations: "When Rabbi Meir...," "When Kalman...," "The sun rose...," pp. 20, 21 and 30-31, from David Roskies, *Night Words*, Copyright (c) 1971 B'nai B'rith Hillel Foundations, Washington, D.C. Reprinted with permission.

Christian Science Monitor: Excerpt from "A story of courage ..," by Kristin Helmore, in *The Christian Science Monitor*, May 7, 1985. Reprinted by permission from *The Christian Science Monitor*, Copyright (c) 1985, The Christian Science Publishing Society. All rights reserved.

Cornwall Books: "From Vilna Went Forth Still Another Decree," "Warsaw," and "The Silent Partner," from Aaron Kramer, *A Century of Yiddish Poetry*, Cornwall Books, Copyright (c) 1989. Used with permission.

Education Department of The Workmen's Circle: "Unter Di Khurves Fun Poyln," from *Mir Trogn A Gezang!* by Eleanor Mlotek, p. 192, published by The Workmen's Circle Education Department, New York, Copyright (c) 1972. Used with permission. "Es Brent," p. 12, "Where Shall I Go?" p. 16, " Gib A Brokhe Tsu Dayn Kind," p. 18, "Kadish," p. 39, "Shtiler, Shtiler," p. 46, "They Call Me Zhamele," p. 64, "Zog Nit Keynmol," p. 94, "Am Yisroel Khay!" p. 96, from *We Are Here* by Eleanor Mlotek and Malke Gottlieb, published by the Workmen's Circle Education Department, New York, Copyright (c) 1983. Used with permission.

Farrar, Straus and Giroux, Inc.: Excerpts from *O The Chimneys* by Nelly Sachs, Copyright (c) 1967 by Farrar, Straus and Giroux, Inc. Reprinted by permission of Farrar, Straus and Giroux, Inc. Excerpts from *The Seeker* by Nelly Sachs, Copyright (c) 1970 by Farrar, Straus and Giroux, Inc. Reprinted by permission of Farrar, Straus and Giroux, Inc.

Abraham Foxman: "The greater part...," "Let us not...," and "On September 1, 1943..." from his article in *Journal of Social Studies*, Vol.XX, No. 1, Fall/Winter 1962. Used by permission of the author.

Gefen Publishing House: "Questions and Answers," by Abe Weiss, from *Survivors Speak Out*, a collection by non-professional writers who were survivors of the Holocaust, Copyright (c) Gefen, Jerusalem, 1985. Reprinted with permission.

Holocaust Library: "First ignored...," p. 114, by Elie Wiesel in Irving Abrahamson, ed., *Against Silence, The Voice and Vision of Elie Wiesel*, Copyright (c) 1985 by Holocaust Library, New York. Reprinted with permission.

Henry Holt and Company: "You think you're..." in *Gates of the Forest* by Elie Wiesel, translated by Frances Frenaye, published by Holt, Rinehart and Winston, Inc., 1966, Copyright (c) Henry Holt and Company. Permission granted by Henry Holt and Company. "At Auschwitz...," and "Perhaps some day..." from *Legends Of Our Time* by Elie Wiesel, published by Holt, Rinehart and Winston, 1968.

Copyright (c) Henry Holt and Company. Permission granted by Henry Holt and Company.

Jewish Historical Commission: "In Cracow...," by Julian Gross and "I spent...," by Esther Garfinkel in *Documents of Crime and Martyrdom*, published by the Jewish Historical Commission, Cracow, 1945. "I became separated...," "In March 1943...," "The local community...," by Carola Sapetowa in Noah Griss, *Children's Martyrdom*, published by the Central Jewish Historical Commission, 1947. Reprinted by permission of the Jewish Institute of History in Poland.

Jewish Labor Bund: "The year is 1941...," "A cacophony of wailing...," "Just imagine Chanele...," from *Five Years in the Warsaw Ghetto* by Bernard Goldstein, Copyright (c) 1947 Unser Tsait-Jewish Labor Bund. Used with permission.

Judaism: "There emerges what..." by Emil Fackenheim and "This is what..." by Elie Wiesel in "Jewish Values in the Post-Holocaust Future," in *Judaism*, Vol. 16, No. 3, Summer 1967, pp. 272-3 and 299. Reprinted with permission.

Macmillan Publishing Company: "In the midst...," from *Scroll of Agony: The Warsaw Diary of Chaim A. Kaplan* translated by Abraham I. Katsh, Copyright (c) 1965 Abraham I. Katsch. Reprinted by permission of Macmillan Publishing Company. "At no time...," p.147, reprinted with permission of Charles Scribner's Sons, an imprint of Macmillan Publishing Company from *Man's Quest for God*, by Abraham J. Heschel. Copyright (c) 1954 Abraham Joshua Heschel; Copyright renewed (c) 1982 Hannah Susannah Heschel and Sylvia Heschel.

McFarland and Co.: "There was a question...," "The God who permitted...," and "...our theology became," from *Self Portrait of a Holocaust Survivor*, pp. 149-50, Copyright (c) 1985 by Werner Weinberg. Reprinted by permission of McFarland and Company, Inc., Publishers, Jefferson, N.C.

Maurice Meier: "We were the...," "Tiengen was a peaceful...," "Unlike most villages...," "The first hint...," "In the course...," "Day after day...," "One of our non-Jewish...," "Terrified I went...," from *Refuge* by Maurice Meier, W.W. Norton, Copyright (c) 1962, Maurice Meier. Used with permission of the author.

New American Library: "...would give warnings...,"

p. 162, "There was a small...," p. 163, "Being here seemed...," p. 314, " The sorority girls...," p. 315, "After I got...," "My husband...," "I can look...," p. 317, "A kind of sadness...," "I have a close friend...," p. 318, "I love Israel...," p. 320, from *Voices Of The Holocaust* edited by Sylvia Rothchild. Copyright (c) 1981 by the William E. Wiener Oral History Library of the American Jewish Committee. Reprinted by arrangement with New American Library, a division of Penguin Books U.S.A. Inc., New York, New York. Reprinted by permission.

New Politics: "As a courier...," "I remember ...," "Mordekai Honey sat...," by Jacob Celemenski in *New Politics*, Volume III:4, Number 12, Fall 1964. Reprinted with permission from New Politics.

N.Y. Times: "As a holocaust survivor..." from "The Survivor's Duty is Not to Forget," by Ruth Minsky Sender, March 27, 1988 (Long Island Opinion), *N.Y. Times*. Reprinted with permission.

NYU Press: "I was asked...," and "The Germans...," pp. 28-32, by Marion P. van Binsbergen Pritchard; "I was sixteen...," "Suddenly in November...," and "The camp commandant...," pp. 75-77, by Ivo Herzer; "The warning...," "The money...," "The following night...," and "There were thousands...," pp. 90- 95, by Leo Goldberg; "Originally there were...," "We came to...," and "Then in 1942...," pp. 117-8, by Hanne Liebmann; "The victims perished...," p. 125, by Elie Wiesel, reprinted by permission of New York University Press from *The Courage to Care*, edited by Carol Rittner and Sondra Myers. Copyright (c) 1986 by New York University.

Oberlin College Press: Excerpts from "What's Not in the Heart," and "My Little Sister," pp. 29, 72-3 and 79-80 in *My Little Sister and Selected Poems* by Abba Kovner, FIELD Translation Series, Oberlin College Press, Copyright (c) 1986 Oberlin College Press. Reprinted by permission of Oberlin College Press.

Pantheon Books: "...the bodies weren't burned...," pp. 11-12, "As people reached...," p. 124, "At the gas chamber...," p. 126, "He is terribly...," p. 189, from *Shoah* by Claude Lanzmann, Copyright (c) 1985 by Claude Lanzmann. Reprinted by permission of Pantheon Books, a division of Random House, Inc. "America's response...," p. 311, "In the end...," "Callousness...," p. 313, "Most American intellectuals...," p. 320, "Most newspapers...," p. 321,

"American mass-circulation...," p. 322, "Stong currents...," p.327, "What could the...," p. 331, "A campaign...," p. 333, "Stong pressure needed...," p. 332, "Much more effort...," p. 333, "The measures taken...," p. 334, "There was a moral...," "It was not...," p. 339, from *Abandonment of the Jews: America and the Holocaust 1941-1945*, by David S. Wyman. Copyright (c) 1984 by David S. Wyman. Reprinted by permission of Pantheon Books, a division of Random House, Inc.

Paulist Press: "It is really...," p. 111, from *Conversation with Elie Wiesel* by Harry James Cargas, Copyright (c) 1976 by Paulist Press. Used by permission of Paulist Press.

Personal Interviews, statements and private letters: I am grateful to Rudy Appel, Irving Adler, Allegra Korman, Trude Neu Noack, and Harry and Helen Prus for sharing their personal experiences with me and for giving me permission to print them here.

Przedborzer Association: "In my village...," pp. 45-6 by Bronia Davner-Kesselman, "When the people...," p. 69 by Haim Gershonovitz from *Przedborz Memorial Book*, Tel Aviv, 1977. Used with permission of the Przedborzer Association.

Rabbinical Assembly: "Remember the mutilated...," p. 838, "...remember the slain...," "...help us to continue...," p. 839 reprinted from *Siddur Sim Shalom*, edited by Rabbi Jules Harlow, published by The Rabbinical Assembly and The United Synagogue of America, Copyright (c) by The Rabbinical Assembly. Reprinted by permission.

Random House: "One has to be mad...," p. 79 from *Zalman, or the Madness of God* by Elie Wiesel, translated by Nathan Edelman. Copyright (c) 1975 by Elie Wiesel. Reprinted by permission of Random House, Inc.

Russel and Volkening: "We who are...," p. 19 from Yaffa Eliach, ed., *Hasidic Tales of the Holocaust*, Oxford University Press, 1982. Reprinted by permission of Russell and Volkening as agents for the author, Copyright (c) 1982 by Yaffa Eliach. Reprinted with permission.

Summit Books: "You who live...," p. 11, "On the morning...," "All took leave...," "When all was ready...," "Dawn came...," pp. 14-16, "...for the first...," "I have learnt...," pp. 26-27, "Death begins with...," pp. 34-5, "The distribution...," p. 39, "...we

have learnt...," p. 55, "One can hear...," "So our nights...," pp. 61-3, "Jan. 18...," pp. 151-173 and 181-184, "I returned to Auschwitz...," pp. 386-7 from Primo Levi, *Survival in Auschwitz—The Reawakening*, copyright (c) 1986 by Summit Books. Reprinted by permission of Summit Books, a division of Simon and Schuster, Inc.

SUNY Press: "After Auschwitz...," and "Every age...," p. xi from *Legacy of Night*, Copyright (c) 1982. Reprinted by permission of the State University of New York Press.

University of Pittsburgh Press: "The final solution...," p. 96, "Too weak...," p. 47, "Near the crematoria...," p. 92, "I don't know...," p. 113, reprinted from *In Evidence: Poems of the Liberation of Nazi Concentration Camps*, by Barbara Helfgott Hyett, by permission of the University of Pittsburgh Press. (c) 1986 by Barbara Helfgott Hyett.

Vallentine and Mitchell: "One day at the end...," p.117, Roni Alshech (Yael Shemtov) in Ze'ev Hadari and Ze'ev Tsahor, *Voyage to Freedom*. Copyright (c) Vallentine and Mitchell, London, 1985. Used with permission.

Vanguard Press: "...as soon as...," "In the center...," p. 186, "The SS led...," "Bitterly the women...," p. 187, "Then I began...," "I was part...," p. 189, "There were...," p. 191 from *Night Of The Mist*, by Eugene Heimler. Copyright (c) 1959 by Eugene Heimler. Reprinted by permission of Vanguard Press, a division of Random House, Inc.

Elie Wiesel: "During the holocaust..." by Elie Wiesel from *Newsday*, November 8, 1988. Reprinted with permission of Elie Wiesel.

OTHER SOURCES

Samuel Rajzman and Abraham Lissner in Yuri Suhl, *They Fought Back*, Crown Publishers, N.Y., 1967.

Vladka Meed and Anonymous participant in Katz and Ringelheim, eds., *Proceedings of the Conference on Women Surviving: The Holocaust*, Institute for Research in History, N.Y., 1983.

Ziff-Davis: "One day a selectee...," p. 154, reprinted from *Five Chimneys: The Story of Auschwitz*, by Olga Lengyl translated by Clifford Coch and Paul Weiss, Copyright (c) 1947 by Ziff-Davis Publishing Company.

Book Design: Robert J. O'Dell